Out of the Bubble

Shelby McGrath Myers

Table of Contents

Acknowledgements

How can I ever properly express my gratitude? So many individuals, some whose names I will never know, have given so much to my family. I have been blessed with such an extraordinary support system and I believe that you are only as strong as the support which you are shown - mine has made me whole. The acknowledgements are endless, but I will try to recognize as many as possible. For those whose names I will never know, but can recall the kind deeds which they so selflessly gave, I can only say thank you.

Ultimately, this book is dedicated to my family and friends. To my children, whose lives were turned upside down, but yet became compassionate beyond their years. They amaze me every day and it is from them I continue to learn and grow. To my husband, who remained strong when I needed to be weak, worked tirelessly so that I could stay home and, mostly, gave me 5 little souls that I could never love more. Thank you for loving me, especially when I was not easy to love. To my parents, who changed their lives, to give our children a sense of normalcy (against incredible odds), and did more for us than I could possibly list -

thank you, for holding my hand and never letting it go. To my

brother and extended family, for their love and support, you are very

appreciated and loved. To my friends, both new and those who have

stood by me for years, I can never thank you for all that you have

done.

I would fall short on acknowledgements if I did not mention

those individuals within Children's Hospital of Philadelphia,

Newborn Nurses and Holly Dell School. There are so many names,

that I don't want to select a random few. I was touched by the

outpouring of support, guidance and compassion. My son was never

treated as a patient, but more so as a sick child. They listened, were

interested and, mostly, allowed me to be a parent. They cried with

me and triumphed at Clay's miracles. They cared, instead of just

caring for my son.

To all of the nameless faces who prayed, hoped and loved my

family. You showed us the meaning of generosity, one which I will

try each day to show to others.

Lastly, I not only would like acknowledge, but dedicate this

memoir to my son Clayton. It is every parent's dream that their children make a difference in this world, and he continues to do so each day, even though he is only with me in spirit. He showed me the meaning of hope, the importance of family and friends, and unconditional love. He made a lasting impression on all those privileged to meet him and his story serves as inspiration. Clayton will always be with me and continues to live in all that I do and achieve.

Forward

I am a parent, who lived, continues to live and survived an experience without words. I am inviting you into my world within these pages, and the lives of my family, to allow you a glimpse of an ordinary life during extraordinary times.

My goal with writing this book was to convey my journey, as a parent within a crisis situation, resulting in a new normalcy. If you are experiencing a similar situation, I am not offering you solutions within these pages -I simply hope that you will know that you are not alone and that your emotions have been felt by another. I am a Mommy, not a medical professional, so these words are from my heart and not case studies.

My hope is that this book will be read by professionals dealing with parents within the hospital setting and home. Parents need support and resources, before being expected to advocate for their sick child. I hope that this book will offer a glimpse of life behind a diagnosis and how an extended hospital stay can psychologically affect family dynamics.

I must add before you begin this book, that it is written in the first person therefore, the word "I" is utilized throughout the pages. By no means would my story be complete without prefacing that "I" was not and, am not, living the story alone. My husband, my children, my parents, our families and so many others are involved and their thoughts and feelings should not go unmentioned. They suffered the pain, rejoiced in the triumphs and continue to ache for the loss of Clayton.

Clayton 2 weeks before the virus

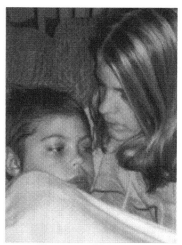

Clayton and Mommy
1st night home

Clayton and Daddy
1st time back to the beach

Our family
2010

" Clayton the Great"
March 2012

Due to your purchase, a cure for Epilepsy will be closer. A portion
of the proceeds from the sale of "Out of the Bubble" will be donated
to our organization, Clayton's Hope (a non-profit which funds
Epilepsy research, awareness and support).
www.claytonshope.org

The Unimaginable

I always told my children how fortunate they were. They were blessed with a loving family, while others were not as lucky. I taught them to look out for others, to be compassionate, to be cognizant of the feelings of others and to watch out for those who were in need. Bullying was never an acceptable behavior and "potty talk" was a lengthy list of words not to be spoken.

Our lives were that of the typical suburban family. We encountered bumps in the road, but nothing that was not settled by the next morning. Struggles occurred, but we managed to overcome the obstacles (which looking back now were more overcast skies than tsunamis). The days never seemed to have enough hours, my car was always on its way somewhere, money never seemed to stretch far enough and bedtimes were interesting. But, at the end of the day we had our health and family. Our lives were complete and we were happy. Little did we know that everything which we held dear was about to change forever. I can vividly remember every detail, although, it has been eight years (at the time which I am writing this book). It is a peculiar thing that one can remember details of a tragic event years later: I could not tell you what I had for breakfast this morning, but the memories of this time in my life

1

are embedded in my soul.

The "unimaginable" experience began with a typical week in mid -October; a month signified with a multitude of back to school errands, and the task of selecting Halloween costumes. The costume process was an adventure and I still hadn't taken the children to get them even though they had been asking since August. Our oldest child, Ashley, was then 11, an age in which she wanted something "cool" for a costume. Clayton, our middle child was still at an easy age (six), and a costume could be purchased with ease (I was still able to convince him of a costume that was available); although, this year he insisted on being a ninja. Our youngest, Ashton, was only nine months, so a hand-me-down costume would be the way to go. The costume selection process was always an ordeal, but a tradition in my home. We would head to the store, knowing I would referee at least one fight in the car, stand for an hour while they selected their costume (and then change their minds), talk them out of the costume that was completely out of the price range and, ultimately, everyone went home happy. I love traditions and this year, unknowingly, would miss them terribly.

Upon waking Clayton for school, on Tuesday, October 14th,

I noticed that he had a fever. Clay was typically our early riser, so having to wake him was never a good sign. He complained that he wasn't feeling well and I attributed it to a back to school bug. So I did what occurs each time one of the kids are sick - I grabbed the Motrin, a supply of pillows for the couch and a cold rag. I explained to Ashley that her brother wasn't faking being sick and attempted to keep Ashton from tackling his brother. As the day progressed, Clay was getting back to his chipper self and the normal routines progressed.

By that evening, the usual chaos transpired in our home - nothing out of the ordinary. Dinner was prepared, Clay and Ashton were wrestling on the floor and Ashley played her video games. My husband arrived home from work, baths were given and the bedtime rituals took place (bedtimes never meant that my children actually went to sleep, but it was a nice thought that tonight would be different).

I ran out to the pharmacy to get Motrin once everyone had settled, in the event Clay's fever resurfaced during the night. Heading down the aisle I spotted a Ninja costume hanging on the rack. It was Clay's size and exactly what he wanted for Halloween.

I remember thinking how wonderful it was that an additional item was checked off my list unexpectedly. As I got closer to the garment, I noticed that the photograph on the front looked exactly like Clay - now I definitely had to purchase it! He would love it and unknowingly at the time I would realize the importance of that purchase. At that moment, I just knew that the smile on his face would be priceless, so, I grabbed my bags and headed home, hopefully to a quiet house.

The night was peaceful. Clay slept in our bed so I could keep an eye out and Ashton got up only once. I awoke thinking that all was well, but my thinking was stopped short. My kids have internal thermometers, seriously, as soon as a fever begins their ears turn red - Clay's ears were purple. I let him stay in bed until I settled Ashley for school and Ashton had breakfast, then I got Clay comfortable on the couch. It would be another day off from school, so the phone calls began to his school and pediatrician. His doctor wasn't worried, probably one of the fall "bugs," so I decided to keep an eye out and "Dr. Mom" would keep him comfortable. Clay was never one to sit still for any length of time, so for him to sleep most of the day meant that he wasn't feeling well at all. I loaded him with

Gatorade, applied and reapplied cold compresses and alternated Tylenol and Motrin, and finally by the afternoon his fever broke. Clay wanted to play video games and all seemed well in the world again.

By dinner, though, Clay was back on the couch, by his own undertaking – this was also never a good sign. I grabbed the thermometer and sure enough his fever was back up. More cold compresses, a mom assessment for a listing of any aches and pains, Motrin - he was back to sleep within 10 minutes. I began the evening routines; clean up dinner, settle everyone down, get Ashton dressed for bed. Then came a moment that I will relive, question and feel guilt for the rest of my life - Clay began to scream. He sat straight up on the couch, eyes opened (but not focused on anything) and was continuously screaming. I held him tight thinking that he was having a nightmare (which he sometimes did in the middle of the night), but this was different. He calmed down after a couple of minutes and I held him close, but he was not coherent. He began to babble, not really making much sense and had no idea who he was or where he was. I screamed for Ashley to hand me the phone. My hands were on the buttons to dial 911 when he stopped and fell back to sleep. He was still feverish, but calm, so I opted to call the pediatrician in lieu of the ambulance. I took Clay's temperature prior to dialing the phone and it was 105.6! I contacted the pediatrician, with whom I had already been on the phone with earlier in the day, and explained in detail the events which had just transpired. He asked if Clay's neck hurt (I now know he was ruling out meningitis) and told me that a fever was just the body's way of fighting a virus. I was told that I *could* take him to the emergency room if I felt it necessary, but felt as though it was not emergent based on the physician's response. I let him know that I would wait until my husband got home in an hour and we would assess the situation at that point. I administered Motrin, cold rags and didn't move until Clayton began to stir. He awoke sweating profusely just as Tim, my husband, arrived home. Fortunately his fever had also broken. I ran through the events of the evening and we decided to see how the next hour would progress before waiting in an emergency room for three hours.

Within a half hour Clay was sitting up and chatting away with Tim and his siblings. His fever had dropped to 100 degrees and he was able to get down some liquids. My heart was still racing, but

Clayton seemed to have had an instant recovery. A shower always seemed to make the kids feel better, so Clay played in the shower and I let him stay in longer than usual for the steam to help with any congestion. It worked and Clay was happily sitting up on the couch chatting away and even eating. Whatever had happened had left as fast as it arrived. We opted not to go to the hospital, but to put him in our bed and try to get some rest, though I don't think that I slept.

Morning came and Clay's fever was only a little above normal. Still, I felt that a trip to the pediatrician's was necessary based on the events of the night before, so I scheduled an appointment for later that morning. I can still recall a conversation that Clay and I had in the kitchen that day and how it was almost foreshadowing. I was making coffee, probably my second pot after not sleeping much the prior evening, and Clay walked up to me with a puzzled look on his face. "Hi, munchkin," I said, "how are you feeling?" "Mommy, did you tell Daddy last night that you were going to take me to the hospital if my fever didn't go away?" Clay asked. "Yes I did, sweetheart. You had a really high fever and we were worried about you." Clay looked at me wide-eyed and said,

"Do I still need to go?" "No," I replied, "but we do need to go to the doctor's to have you checked out." With that he walked away. Giving me no fight about going to the doctors, I thought he must not be feeling well. I went back to my coffee and he went to play with Ashton, life was back to normal, so I thought.

The doctor's office was uneventful. I was sure that Clay would have strep or an ear infection based on his high fever, but nothing was out of the ordinary. In fact, the only difference in Clay was that he was a little lethargic from being sick. His temperature was normal, no antibiotics were needed and he seemed to be on the mend. I actually felt a little silly about my reactions on the last telephone conversation with the pediatrician, looking at this healthy child sitting in the office. At least I knew that it was nothing major and we headed home. I contacted Tim and let him know that his "little man" was fine. I was in contact with my mother the prior evening via telephone knowing she would probably be worried being five states away visiting my brother, so I called with the "all clear." I could breathe, so I thought, and went back to the accumulation of wash that was taking over my home (if I don't do at least a load a day, I am sunk- it had been about three since a single load had been cleaned). I called Clay's school and relayed the update to them and added that I would probably just keep Clay out to rest the following day since it was Friday.

Back to the Halloween costume. Clay came into my room when I was folding my fifth load of laundry after dinner and wanted to try on his costume. Typically, I make the kids wait until Halloween to put their costumes on, with the fear that something will rip and we will have to make another purchase, but he looked at me so pleadingly and said, "please, Mommy." Thankfully, I responded yes, to his pleas and he eagerly put on his Ninja outfit. He paraded around the house and made sure that Tim saw him in his very "cool" attire. Clay was having a hard time adjusting to the full day of first grade and being separated from me all day, so it didn't come as too much of a surprise when he repeatedly asked if I would be at the parade. I was not going to be in the room for dress up time, though, and he was very concerned that the other Mommy's would not know how to adjust the outfit correctly. I assured him that all would be fine - not knowing that it wouldn't. This would be the only time that I would see my "little Ninja" in his costume and Halloween would not come for him this year. Thankfully, he asked to put on the Ninja costume that night and I am even more thankful that higher powers must have aided my response.

That evening Clay was up later than usual; he was always my "sleeper," so it was a little uncommon. I asked him what was wrong and I will never forget the conversation that would follow. He asked me, "Mommy, what is heaven like?" I looked him in the eyes with a grapefruit sized lump in my throat and chills running down my spine. "Well, I have never been there Clay, so I am really not sure." I was hoping this conversation would end with this statement because I was suddenly very scared, but it did not. "Mommy," Clay repeated, "What is heaven like?" "Clay, are you worried about something, are you worried that something will happen to Mommy?" "Yes," he replied. Not knowing that this conversation was more important than I would ever realize, I replied, "Well, Heaven is the most beautiful place in the world. It has everything that you could ever want." I was hoping that this would end our talk, but it continued. Clay responded, "Mommy, how do you get there?" Now, I was beyond worried as Clay had never brought this subject up prior to this night. "Well, everyone that loves you, even those people who you have never met will come and get you. They will keep you safe until Mommy and Daddy are with you again, but don't worry nothing is going to happen to you or us. I promise you that I will always be here with you." The tears began to flow. The tears are continuing to flow as I am now writing this. I think that Clay knew something was going on and I hope that this conversation gave him peace when he needed it. I hope that I relayed the answers in a way that he understood, but I will never know.

Friday, October 15th would be the last day that we would have with "Clayton" as a healthy 6-year-old boy. The day started normal, as it was the first day all week that Clay awoke without a fever. I kept him home from school, due to the 24 hour "fever free" policy that our school instates, but he seemed to be healthy and happy. It was the normal chaotic morning of breakfast, Ashley catching the bus, feeding Ashton and catching up on laundry.

By lunchtime, Clay was itching to get out of the house, so I told him that we could take a short ride to Subway and get some sandwiches to drop off to Tim. Ashton and Clayton were playing in the car, life was good. We dropped off sandwiches and Clay even bounded out of the car to give Tim his lunch.

The rest of the day was uneventful and by dinner

pandemonium had settled back into our household. Normal conversations were taking place, "Clay please don't play so rough with Ashton." "Please pick up your toys before I break my neck on them!" and of course, "No more snacks or you will never eat your dinner." I got dinner on; Ashton settled and turned to find Clay lying on the couch. He was flushed and feverish. I figured that it was just from playing hard after being sick all week, so I gave Motrin and settled him down with a movie.

Clay fell asleep on the couch that night and I remember sitting down with him and holding him in my arms. Ashton awoke and I asked Tim to carry Clay into our bed so that I could get Ashton to sleep. If I had known what would happen only six hours later, I would have held him all night. But, I had no idea, nor could I ever foretell something so horrific was about to happen.

I awoke and glancing at my clock on the night stand beside my side of the bed saw that it was 3:15 a.m. and my bed was soaked. Clay was lying next to me and had saturated our bed. During the week he was sick with fever, this had happened a couple of times, so I wasn't that concerned. Although the other times I kept him in our room and got him changed and got us resituated, I am not sure why this time in particular I chose to walk him into his room to his own bed. I have questioned this choice since that night. Maybe, someone was aiding me, because I am not sure what would have happened had I not chose this option.

I remember taking him into his room and he was not walking steadily, but I had just woke him up, so I presumed it was because he was not fully awake. He staggered and while trying to get him changed he was extremely stiff and not answering me. I yelled for Tim to come in - something was not right. At the moment Tim entered the room, Clay turned and jumped into his bed. I thought that odd (normally he would have whined to come back into our room), but it was the middle of the night, so Tim and I assumed he was not coherent due to still being half asleep. Tim chose to sleep in Clay's room with him, so gave them both a kiss and left the room.

I went into the kitchen to grab something to drink, threw Clay's clothes into the hamper and remember having a horrible feeling that something was not right. I felt the need to go back and check on Clay and as I approached the door I knew something was wrong before I even got the door opened. The room was dark and Tim was lying next to him. I asked Tim if Clay was alright and he said "I think so - he's sleeping." I went over to touch his face. His back was to Tim and I could see in the moonlight that Clay's eyes were wide open, but he wasn't moving! I flicked on the light and we saw him lying motionless, eyes wide and drooling profusely. Clay wouldn't respond. Tim scooped him up and I ran to call 911. I don't remember the call or what exactly happened next. I just remember the ambulance arriving and Clay sitting on my lap at the dining room table. His eyes were shut now and he was sleeping, but would not wake up. I thought that he had suffered a stroke, but soon learned that he had suffered a seizure.

I rode in the ambulance with Clay, Tim situated the kids with my father and before I knew it we were in the emergency room trying to decipher what had just transpired. He received a CAT scan (which was normal), IV fluids and he seemed comfortable. We were told that he probably had a febrile seizure. Although he had had one previously from a ruptured ear drum at the age of one, Tim and I both knew this seizure was different. They began to bring up options regarding which hospitals were better equipped to treat pediatric patients as this hospital did not have a pediatric neurology department. All was still moving at a slow pace and my nerves were actually calming a bit. Clay looked very peaceful, therefore there seemed to be no urgency and no outward signs of concern from the doctors.

Upon recounting the events to one more doctor, I stood and watched Clay seize again. The atmosphere in the room changed dramatically. More doctors came in and we now had to make a choice as to which pediatric hospital to transport him and emergency medications were being administered. Nurses were making calls and they were rushing to get Clay situated on a stretcher for transport - I felt as though I was watching a movie, I was numb. Then, I began to cry and for a moment the severity of the situation was evident. They were taking away my son, my baby- what was happening?

We chose to have Tim ride with Clay this time. I was going home first to check on the kids and get some of Clay's favorite animals. I don't remember driving home; although, I remember very clearly what happened when I arrived. Ashton was playing with my dad and Ashley was on the computer. I furnished my dad with a quick update, gathered Clay's favorite animals and went in to see Ashley. She looked up, I gave her a hug and told her that Clay was alright and promised that I would bring him home. I will never forget that conversation, the look in her eyes, or the impact of those words.

I jumped in the car and got on the phone. I would like to say that I wasn't talking and driving, but I was and I don't even remember the trip to the hospital. I recall calling my mother (she was still in New Hampshire and desperately trying to get home at that point) and I called my sister-in-law and asked for prayers to be started. I cried, prayed, remembered and tried not to think too much. I got lost, but somehow found my way and pulled into the hospital. I would never leave the same again, nor would Clay or our family. I would leave a part of myself outside of those doors, the memory of a life we would no longer have and a child's soul that we would lose. I had absolutely no idea, nor could I ever imagine the journey we were all about to encounter. Knowledge, heartbreak, compassion and every possible emotion awaited me, but all I would know at that point was that my child was waiting for me and I was on my way.

In the Beginning

I recall arriving at the hospital and upon navigating my way and finding Clay, feeling relieved. We were at one of the best hospitals in the world and it all seemed very surreal. Clay was sleeping and looked extremely peaceful and healthy. Tim was giving the doctors the necessary information and no one seemed overly concerned. The morning's events were reiterated about 5 times to different faces that entered his room, and the atmosphere was very relaxed.

I placed Clay's favorite stuffed animals on his bed and began the task of answering countless questions. We were never in a hospital with our children, except for their birth and stitches, so this was unfamiliar and intimidating at times.

Clay had not had a seizure since we arrived and I began to wonder if maybe the need was as emergent as we first suspected, to be at a hospital (much less one in another state). I began the necessary phone calls; we arranged for Tim's mom to help my father with the kids, I contacted my mother (who was desperately trying to get a flight home from visiting my brother) and contacted my aunt (who was coming up to the hospital to give us some moral support). I was in desperate need of air, so I navigated my way outside. It was a beautiful day, warm for October, and not a cloud in the sky. I was numb, hadn't slept more than a couple of hours and none of us had eaten since dinner the night before - so I stopped in the McDonald's within the hospital to grab some food. I stood in line and, of course, ordered the usual Happy Meal for Clay, never imagining he would never eat again.

Upon entering the room, they informed us that Clay would be administered the first of many tests- a spinal tap. I was actually happy that something was being done to give us some answers. The doctor in the emergency room was attributing the morning's events to febrile seizures (which Clay had previously at a year and a half) - I knew this was not the case. The look he had, the lack of response and the fact that he still was not awake was not reassuring me that I was wrong. But, upon administering the test to Clay, he spoke the last word that I would hear from him (without knowing so at this point). "Stop it," he said and then went back to sleep. My heart broke for him, but at the same moment I was thrilled to hear him speak.

It was the afternoon by now, my aunt had arrived and she, Tim, my father-in-law and I were standing in Clay's room. The doctors were coming in and out and we were in a holding pattern. The tests, so far, had come back normal and the doctor on more than one occasion told me that all seemed fine. Fine - I looked over and Clay had another seizure. I broke down and held onto who ever was closest. I felt, no I didn't feel, I was numb. I watched in horror as there was absolutely nothing that I could do for my son. The doctors and nurses came in and no one brought up the word fine again. They administered medication and now, those medications sounded completely unfamiliar. I remember the doctor saying to me, "See if you can wake him up." I didn't even realize until that point that he was supposed to be awake. So I went over to the bed, took Clay in my arms and began to talk to him. He didn't respond, he didn't wake up and the mood in the room began to change. Now, the doctors were talking about the ICU - Clay would be admitted. Admitted, to the hospital, what in the world was happening? Still, I was holding it together, we were in the hospital and hospitals always make children better. Never once did it occur to me that anything else could be possible.

They wheeled Clay; sound asleep with his stuffed animals accompanying him, up to the ICU. Monitors and an IV were attached to him and we stood and watched. We met the doctors on the floor, who informed us what would be happening, they would watch Clay and we would let them know if we saw anything. 'Saw anything,' I recall thinking, "aren't *you* the doctor"? All was well, we didn't see anything, and he just slept. My parents arrived and I recall my mother saying how peaceful he looked - he did. Thankfully, they brought us something to eat; we made some calls, checked on the kids and my parents left to be with Ashley and Ashton. Little did we know those moments would be the last normal moments I would have for the rest of my life.

About an hour after my parents left, Clay began to seize. We let the nurse know and she informed us that it was not a seizure - it was *indeed* a seizure. Clay pursed his lips, twitched them to the side and began to drool profusely. Even on that first night, he began to teach people. The doctor came in and I held Clay in my arms, stroked his hair and tried to talk to him to calm him down. I told him how much I loved him, said out loud his favorite foods and things to do - it didn't work. He kept seizing and the doctors kept administering more medication. Tim and I stood and watched as they shoved things in his mouth to help with the drool and tried to make the seizures stop, but instead they were coming closing together and more profound. The doctor asked us to step outside of the room.

I sat in a chair outside of Clay's room and held his favorite dog, hugging it as if it was my son. We were informed that Clay's condition could go one of two ways, the seizures would stop or they would have to intubate him due to the sedation of the medication (if more needed to be administered). Then, we heard the monitors in the room, Clay's oxygen was dropping due to the medication and before we knew it - our son was on a ventilator. He couldn't be monitored on an EEG (a device which measures brain waves and abnormalities) on the floor that he was on, so he was moved to the new PICU at 2 a.m. on October 16, 2004. This new room would be the room of a new child by the time we left.

As the early hours of the morning progressed, all became quiet. Clay was so sedated that he was not breathing on his own. And so, the monitors were the only sounds and the only sign that we had that Clay was alright. I called home a couple of times during the night to give updates, which got progressively worse as the night wore on. We met his new nurses and doctors and I laid down at about 4 a.m. to sleep - Tim stayed up and kept watch. I don't think that I dreamt, but I know that I didn't want to wake up, or should I say, I wanted to wake up at home with my son in my arms. I didn't, but while half asleep, I heard someone talking to Clay. The person kept calling him, "Buddy," and the way that he spoke, you would think that it was a two way conversation. As I cautiously opened my eyes, it was a reality. My son lay in a hospital bed next to me, tubes and wires attached to him, IV lines in his arms and legs and breathing by a tube down his throat. I don't think I could ever possibly convey the heartbreak that I felt that first morning. I cried and I wanted to get out of the hospital. I wanted to pick up my child and take him home, this was not happening. I, as a Mommy, was supposed to be able to fix everything. We were a normal family, this doesn't happen except on television or in a magazine article. At that moment, I went numb. I saw my child, helpless and I shut down - my emotions anyway. I went into survival mode; this is the only way that I can explain it.

The morning brought "rounds" of the doctors, detailing what would be done, what they were looking for, did we have any questions. Did we have questions? What in the world just happened in the past 24 hours?! What were they going to do and mostly, what could we do? "Wait," is what we were told. Wait, alright, at this point the doctors were god to us, they were going to fix whatever was wrong and we were going to go home. That was obviously our thinking and not their opinion of the situation. So, we called our family and gave updates. I talked to my Mom about Ashley and Ashton and the best way for us all to handle them coming to the hospital. Ashton would stay home and Tim and I would talk to Ashley when she arrived. Talk to Ashley - I really felt as though I was in a movie. Ashley and I had the normal mom and daughter "talks," even the "talks" about more delicate subjects, but how and what were we suppose to tell her? Clay and Ashley were inseparable at home. Sure they disagreed, but they never fought. Many a night, she would sleep in his top bunk, and they would play endlessly during the day. How could I talk to my daughter and watch her face as she saw her brother in this condition? My heart was broken and now it was about to break again - for my children. I would take their place to ease any pain, but I couldn't make this better for her or him. Ashton was too young to understand, he loved his Clay dearly - but luckily, he was too young to realize what was happening.

Ashley arrived with my parents, with a present for Clay. I remember sitting her down outside of Clay's room. Tim and I told her what we knew, the machines that he was on and what was happening. She cried and I held her as hard as I could - I was numb, I didn't cry. I removed myself from the situation, even on this first day, so that I could breathe. I took her by the hand and led her into Clay's room - he looked beautiful as if he was just asleep. We showed her what everything did and she sat next to him on the bed. She was quiet - I think at that moment, she removed herself in order to function.

I really don't remember much about the rest of the day. Tim's family visited, friends called and we made necessary arrangements with my parents for Ashley and Ashton. The doctors told us that in the morning they would lower the sedation, which had given Clay's brain time to "rest," so I believed that all would be well and home would be in the near future. The nightmare would be over and life would be back to normal. I look back now and realize not only how wrong I was, but that possibly I was only taking in what my brain would allow me to process. The visitors left and Tim and I sat in the room next to Clay. Normally, we would be chasing after someone in the house or refereeing an argument. Tim worked extremely long hours, so typically we didn't have nights when we would just sit. Now, we sat in a cold, quiet hospital room - no doctors or visitors, and I began to ache for our life at home. I needed to leave. I wanted to be in our safe haven of home, to recharge, or regroup - maybe just to sit and compose myself. Mostly, I wanted to hold my babies that seemed so far away. Tim and I didn't have clothing or any necessities, so I made the choice that I would leave and gather some belongings. I desperately needed to get out of the hospital. So, I let Tim know that I was going to go home for a little while; Clay would be safe with him, and left.

I hadn't spoken to a number of my friends since Clay was admitted, so I made some brief calls to aid the loneliness of the drive. I was as brief as possible – what I really needed was to just talk about something other than the tragedy of the day. I was actually afraid to drive, as my mind was on so many thoughts that I don't know how I made it home. I pulled up to the house and my mom met me outside, fearing the worst, but I let her know that I just needed to see the kids. I will never forget Ashton that evening and now wonder if it was foreshadowing that occurred. I picked him up and he smiled with joy. He placed both of his little hands on either side of my face and just looked into my eyes and smiled and then held onto me tightly. Now, writing this, I have a lump in my throat because after that night our relationship would change - all of our lives would forever change. But, on this night, all I knew was that I was home. I talked with Ashley for a little while and threw some clothes into a duffle bag. My home was so quiet; no laughter, no television blaring, no fighting, no sound. I walked into Clay's room and just stood and as I did the tears just flowed. I imagined him lying in his bed and the events of the previous day, which now felt like a lifetime ago. Without thinking I sat on his bed, the room was dark and quiet. I grabbed his pillow and realized that I was holding it and rocking, just like I did to make the boo boo's disappear, but this time I couldn't - I just cried. As I sat there and held that pillow tight, for a moment I was with my healthy son. I needed to pretend at that point, no, I needed my son and he wasn't there. He was in the hospital hooked to so many machines and I couldn't stop crying.

I took a breath, composed myself and headed back to my parent's house. Tim and I purchased a home with an in-law suite with my parents a couple of years prior and as I look back now - fate would make this a blessing. Our homes were connected by a wall, each with its own home and entrance, but they were accessible through the basement. In time, the wall would become a doorway, one of many changes to come.

I opened the door and reality was back. My children were with my parents, Clay was nowhere to be found and I had to get back to the hospital - I felt like I was numb, but I wasn't at that moment and I hurt horribly. I wanted to be with my children, that is where their Mommy was supposed to be. I wanted to stay home and pretend that this was not real, but it was and I needed to be with Clay. Looking back, it was such chaos those first two days, I am thankful my parents were so close to our children. They stepped in and gave them exactly what they needed most - love. I don't remember if I gave them instructions, they knew them so well that they just took control. They were there when I couldn't be and keeping things as normal as possible for them. My heart broke, but I needed to leave to go back with Clay. I made sure that my parents had what they needed and tried desperately not to cry. I am sure I
did just that on the ride back to the hospital - I don't remember the ride, just that I had to get back.

The Early Phases

The next morning, October 17th, the doctors expected to remove Clayton from the Pentobarbital coma, and the seizures would be gone. Tim went down to get coffee and I jumped into the shower in Clay's room. It was a sunny day and I remember feeling elated that this nightmare of a week was over. I guess I believed that the medication would come off and Clay would be his healthy self again - I couldn't have been more mistaken.

The doctors lowered the medication and we eagerly anticipated seeing Clay open his eyes. We waited and watched. In horror, we watched Clay's mouth began to twitch, slowly at first and then more pronounced. He opened his eyes, only to stare and continue to seize. The doctors and nurses rushed at this point. They were no longer speaking to us, but to each other in terminology that we didn't understand. What was once a large room became very small, consumed with personnel hurriedly attending to Clay - I froze. I don't remember where Tim was in the room, but I recall looking on as if watching a movie.

The first of many miracles happened at that moment. I was standing against the wall watching in horror the events unfolding.

Nurses were standing in the hallway and I felt someone begin to rub my back. I was consoled and turned to thank this wonderful nurse who showed me such compassion. I turned around to find no one there. I was given a gift and I knew exactly who it was - I felt my grandmother's presence and knew that we were not alone. I was not afraid, I felt peace if only for a moment.

A little while later, I was standing at the head of Clay's bed rubbing his hair and talking to him, when the doctors entered to talk to Tim and I. The strategy did not work as they thought and he would have to be kept in a medicinal coma for an unknown period of time. Their hope was that his brain would "reset." His brain would be given a rest, in hopes that the seizures would end. I felt the tears streaming down my face and I began to cry uncontrollably. I was leaning over Clay at this point hugging him through the breathing tubes and wires and Tim was taking the reins with the doctors. I didn't want to be in control. I wanted to leave. I wanted to unplug my son from all of these machines and take him home. I wanted him to get out of the bed and resume being a 6-year-old little boy. This was not happening - this is the situation of talk show and magazine articles, not our life. I felt completely out of control and my rationality was gone. I was beginning to understand the severity of the situation; although, my brain was not letting me compute the reality of what was transpiring.

The doctors, I am sure now, saw the signs of a parent that was about to snap and told Tim and I to leave. They told us that they would not leave Clay's side and to go get air. They let us know of some places in close proximity to the hospital to grab something to eat - we obeyed. We placed our son in their care and we left. I remember it being a beautiful warm afternoon and the world was normal outside of the hospital. People were going about their everyday activities; they were on lunch breaks, running errands, shopping, and our world was non-existent. We were in limbo and lost. I was numb and felt nothing - not the breeze, not the sun shining on my face. I was walking to lunch, as my son lay on life support, and I wanted to scream. I felt exceedingly guilty that I was able to leave the hospital, to get some time to regroup, while my son did not have that opportunity. Mostly, I felt as though I really wasn't feeling anything - I was going through the motions and not taking anything in. I was on auto pilot.

I don't remember having lunch that day, or even walking

back to the hospital. I do, however, remember entering Clayton's room because it was extremely quiet. The sun was shining through his windows, balloons had arrived from Tim's work and were hanging by his bed and to any passerby - Clay looked like he was peacefully sleeping. I stood and watched my little boy, hooked up to so many machines, and felt very small. I was his mommy and I was supposed to be able to fix all of his boo boos. I had no answers and couldn't do a thing for him. I just watched as they prepared to take him for an MRI and, once again, listened as they instructed us to wait outside of his room. It was at this moment that I was given a gift. I was peering into his room from the hallway and saw my healthy child. The tubes and wires were blocked from my standpoint and all I could see was his tiny face. He looked peaceful, just as he looked so many times that I saw him asleep at home. I could feel the tears streaming down my face and Tim walked over to console me, having no idea what brought on my tears, but knew as soon as I showed him. I prayed for our son to be well and my prayers were answered, the best that they could be at that point in time.

The MRI did not show anything conclusive and Clay steadily declined; although now I am only realizing just how severely. His seizures would not subside, so in addition to the Pentobarbital for his drug induced coma, he was placed on Isoflurane and paralyzed. When the seizures continued to break through, he was placed on Ketamine and finally his brain quieted. His brain was only allowed to have minimal activity, so he was hooked up 24 hours a day to an EEG machine. Due to the countless medications, his blood pressure, and various organs began to be affected. Now, my little boy, whose body only had to tolerate antibiotics until this point in time, was currently on 24 medications. Blood was being drawn so often, that tests had to be lessened due to the amount of Heparin that was administered for blood draws. The doctors let us know that the CDC (Center for Disease Control) had contacted the hospital during the first few weeks to find out what was going on due to the amount and obscure tests that they were ruling out in blood work. Toxicology got involved and screened for anything environmental or toxic that Clay could have come in contact with at home - nothing came back. Tim and I began research and relived the week that he became sick until we just couldn't think anymore. We still had no answers.

Tim and I had our first of many "family meetings" with the doctors and I realized when we were taken to a conference room that this was not good. I also realized that there was a box of tissues in the middle of the table, and this was also not a good sign. We were told that Clay's condition was not improving and that they had never had a child in a drug induced coma for such a long period of time. The doctors were not able to remove him from the coma due to the seizures, so we were at a crossroad. If he did not respond, we would lose him.

Lose him? I became furious! We were in the best hospital in the world and they were supposed to make him well. All of the tests, medications, coma and scans that he had endured were supposed to turn this around, were they not? I remember listening, but computing nothing that was said. We agreed to try a couple of options, but we were persistent in letting them know that our son was fighting; therefore, so would we.

We agreed to have a tracheal tube placed in Clay, so that the intubation tube could be removed from his mouth – we would be able to see his beautiful face. This procedure would also give me the opportunity to hold my son. I did just that a couple of days later. His surgery went well, the tube was removed and after a period of healing I was told that I could hold my baby boy. The nurses helped me onto his bed and moved the countless wires and tubes that were keeping him alive. They placed him on my lap and I held him so very tight. I hugged him and stroked his little face and hair. It seemed like a lifetime since I was able to comfort my son, but yet he was the one comforting me. I cried – tears of joy, sadness, heartache and confusion. The minutes stood still and I looked up to see his nurses crying alongside Tim and I. For that moment I was able to be his Mommy again and I closed my eyes so that I was very far from his hospital room.

Days in the hospital soon turned into weeks and weeks turned into a month. Halloween came and went. I trick-or-treated with my mom and the kids while Tim stayed with Clay. His costume was hanging in his hospital room and I now understood the importance of letting him parade around the house in his costume weeks earlier. My mother had taken Ashley out to get her costume and I wasn't there. One more life event that I wasn't present for during our hospital stay – there would be many. We didn't go home much during the first month, except to work and once or twice a week to visit the kids. My parents would bring them to the hospital to visit on Sundays and my mother would come up on Tuesday nights to visit Clay. Tim and I were "existing" and thankfully, Ashley and Ashton were "living" with my parents.

Time stops in the ICU. There was no definition between day and night, except when looking out of the window it was dark. Tim and I slept on a couch, both of us at either end. We took turns sleeping so that one of us was awake with Clay. When Tim slept was the hardest time. My other children were at home and I felt very much alone. It was during the middle of the night that I learned how special Clay's nurses were - for our well being, as well as his. They would talk to us and listen. We were able to live out our happiest moments by telling the stories of our lives at home. I gained strength by their support and knowledge. Mostly, they treated my son like a sick little boy, not just a patient that was on their shift. I learned that it was alright to cry in front of them and many of them did the same. Clay touched lives in the early phase of his hospital stay, from the nurses to the custodians – people would talk to him as though he was awake. I learned that each member of the hospital staff was an equally intricate part of the healing process and they helped us to exist. They became familiar faces that we would see each day and we welcomed their presence as much as the doctors.

I remember meeting a family during the first couple of weeks whose son had been in the hospital for five months for a heart transplant. Five months! How in the world did they survive? When asked, they told me, "We do what we have to." I had no idea at that moment the importance of that conversation. I didn't understand how they could function away from home for that length of time. How could they be away from their other children for so long and away from their lives? How was it possible to *have* to be in the hospital for so long? I thought that our situation was so different and couldn't fathom Clay being an inpatient for anywhere near that amount of time - I couldn't have been more wrong. I was destined to meet this couple. Over time they would help me more than they would ever know.

I came up with the idea after a couple of weeks to compile a scrapbook, so that Clay would be aware of all the individuals that had helped him. I wanted him to know, when he was well, the generosity supplied by so many people. Mostly, so that when he was well he could see how far he had come. I never let it enter my mind that he would not be well, this wasn't even a hope – it was my way to survive.

Clay's book contained photographs of each of his nurses and doctors - they probably appeased me and thought that I was really losing my mind. But, they smiled for photographs (I would never let Clay be present in the photographs) and even looked at his scrapbook when he was their patient. An outpouring of support and love started to happen from our community all of which went into the scrapbook, as well. A dear friend organized, with the help of many, meals to be delivered daily to our home. Grocery items were dropped off at the house consisting of everything from diapers to staple items, so that my mother had one less task to complete for our children. The newspaper ran stories, we agreed to be interviewed, and donations came pouring into a fund that was set up for our family. We learned that a number of waitresses in our town donated their tips, Girl Scout/Boy Scout troops made signs for Clay's room and even the littlest of children were collecting pennies for Clay.

One day in mid-November, Tim received a phone call from a woman who read the story of Clay in the newspaper. Her daughter had passed away and she wanted to donate the remaining funds from funeral donations, to our family. I remember receiving this phone call from Tim and my heart sank. This woman had just lost her

39

child, and in her grief, was reaching out to help our little boy and his siblings. I cried and I could tell in Tim's voice that he had done the same. There was nothing that we were able to do to ease her pain, or verbalize our gratitude, so we sent her a letter with photographs of our family. I wanted to let her know that when Clay was better we would tell the story of this remarkable woman and her precious little girl.

On another occasion, we were asked to come down to the front desk because there was a visitor that wanted to speak to us. I was not having a good day and asked Tim to go down to greet whoever was there to visit. Upon arriving in the lobby, Tim was approached by the head of construction for the hospital. Workers were there daily, many of which I would see regularly, and came to know about Clay and his story. The gentleman presented Tim with a check and told him that we were to use it to buy gifts for our children. They did a 50/50 every year and the proceeds benefitted children within the hospital at Christmas. This year, they collectively decided to donate the money to our family – in hopes of delivering a wonderful holiday. I now realize that I was not meant to go down to the lobby that day. That wonderful man was meant to meet Clay's daddy.

I printed off and wrote all of these unforgettable events into the scrapbook, which was becoming quite full, and today I am so very happy that I can recollect on those moments. We were numb, very appreciative, but numb. Today, I am overwhelmed at the generosity that was offered by so many. This is a treasured memento in our home. It teaches our other children the compassion and love that changed our lives.

I look back at those first couple of weeks and my heart breaks for Tim. During the initial crisis period and the heartbreaking weeks that followed, my husband remained strong. I never saw him cry, he instead let me do so constantly. He took the reins when I needed to mentally remove myself. He was calm, while I in turn wanted things done yesterday. His son, the same as mine, was slipping away from us – but, yet he was not the one readily consoled. I now look at fathers, going through a crisis situation and hug them without thinking. How very sad that men are expected not to cry.

Years later I asked Tim why he never cried in front of me and his response was, "Because I was supposed to be strong."

Reality Sets In

Being a parent in the hospital long term, with a critically ill child, was an experience in itself – only those who have lived this life can appreciate the oddities which occur. We were once told by one of Clayton's doctors that there is a term that comes with being in the ICU – ICU psychosis. Whatever the generalization, we were in a group – not one that we wanted membership in, but one that became our lifeline at times.

I am sure that if someone could read my mind during the first month – they would have thought that I was close to the edge. I began to come up with rituals based on Clay's condition. If he had a good test result and I was wearing a certain outfit – I would make sure that the same attire was worn for the next test. When I was waiting for the elevator, if it would stop at a certain floor – all would be well that day. Thankfully, no one was able to see the oddities that occurred, but I learned from other parents years later – it was a standard practice within the ICU.

We began to see familiar faces and the families became part of our family. We knew who the parents were and how their child was doing by the expressions on their faces and body language. A faint smile, tears and utter exhaustion replaced expressions we once saw in the outside world. We would rejoice in our children's tiny triumphs – what once would have been the winning score in a game, was now being able to go an hour without having a seizure. Instead of getting good grades, we rejoiced when our children's lab work was improving. We could just talk – about anything other than the situation at hand. Sometimes, that made all of the difference in a day, especially because our world at home seemed so far away.

I had two other children at home living their lives without me. Tim and I called, but we weren't present and missed many of the milestones. Time stopped in our lives, but in the outside world it continued without us. When I was home – I worried about Clayton and felt guilty that I was not by his side. What if I missed something? What if he awoke, or worse – what if he left us and I was not there with him. At the hospital, I missed Ashley and Ashton and every day activities at home. That place was our life. I cried when I had to leave home and cried when I had to leave the hospital – I was certain that this had to be hell and I felt guilty for feeling that way, as well. When I went home, I was able to pretend – if only for a moment. Clay was just at school and our life was perfect. I would venture out on occasion to have some normalcy and pray that I would not run into anyone that I knew. Meaning well, everyone's first question would be, "How is Clay?" and then, "Have the seizures stopped?" The moment in my pretend world would cease and I was forced back into reality. This probably wasn't the most ideal coping mechanism, but when faced with an impossible situation, it was nice to have a reprieve.

While at the hospital, Tim and I lived for the morning doctors' rounds to signify another day of life for Clay, but not really absorbing the reality of the words. We took in what we could comprehend during these meetings (in the beginning we didn't have our honorary degrees in every specialty covering Clay) and I kept a notepad, so as not to ask the same questions multiple times. We researched responses and lived on sites designated for medical terminology and diagnoses. We also became experts at analyzing facial expressions of the medial personnel. We clung to words such as, "tomorrow" and "next week" and the most important, "home." We began to look forward to tests and results, instead of being frightened – maybe something (anything) would be discovered (we were still naïve enough to believe that anything could be cured).

By the end of November Clay's condition had not improved

. It had been six weeks since this nightmare began and there was no end in sight – not one that we would allow to happen anyway. One evening while lying next to Clay, I noticed a reddened area on the back of his neck. Various specialists came in over the course of a couple of days and, after a panel of tests, they found that Clay had an elevated level in his blood consistent of Vasculitis. It was the first test that had come back conclusive of a diagnosis and I actually felt relieved that something had been discovered. If there was a diagnosis, then there had to be a cure – how naïve in my thinking. Vasculitis, as it turned out was not a diagnosis that I would want for Clay.

We met with various teams of doctors – Clay had every specialty reviewing his case at this point (that is not an exaggeration). The prognosis was uncertain, if Clay did in fact have this disease. They would "clean" his blood with a method called plasmapheresis – the plasma would be removed and donated plasma would be transfused into his body. All I heard was "transfusion" – and remember thinking of all of the diseases that he could contract from obtaining donated anything. Also, he would have a month of Cytoxan (a chemotherapy drug) to diffuse the Vasculitis. Tim and I were told that a side effect of the procedure was the possibility of Clay becoming sterile. Sterile - now this was becoming unimaginable. My little boy, who had not even entered puberty, had the possibility of not having children. We had a choice – we chose to do whatever we could to save our son and deal with the future at a later date.

The procedure took place and we waited. Did it work? I really don't know. Clay's seizures continued, but the area on his neck improved and no questionable areas formed on his head. His doctors had mixed reactions to the diagnosis from the start, but they were running out of options (I would later realize). Time was progressing and there was no improvement in sight. They were fighting as hard as we were, probably more so, because they had the tools. I am certain that their frustration level was increasing, so they continued to go over his case in conferences and explored options "outside of the box." The weeks under their care – was now months, with no improvement.

Tim's and my mother's birthday were spent in Clay's hospital room. Thanksgiving Day we went to my uncles. My mother offered to stay with Clay, so that we could spend the holiday as a family, reluctantly we both went. It had been since October that we all ventured anywhere together and it was the first holiday without Clay. I loved the moments with Ashley and Ashton, but I felt numb and as though I was having "visiting time" with my children. I knew when this night was over, so would be this time as a family. Reality would be upon us and we would be back in the hospital with Clay.

Another family meeting was held after the holidays. We were told that Clay could not remain in the coma, but the doctors were suggesting an option to try to stop the seizures. They would perform brain surgery – a corpus callosotomy. During this procedure, the two sides of his brain would be severed by ¾ and would hamper the seizures from becoming generalized (spreading to all areas of his brain). We agreed to meet with the neurosurgeon, neuropsychologist and compile opinions from outside sources. We were told that if the surgery did not work and they were not able to pull Clay from the coma that there was nothing else they could do, we would lose our son.

I went back to his room, stood by the window and cried. I don't remember where Tim went and I think that we both needed to absorb this information in our own way. I felt out of control and couldn't think. I needed air and to get out of Clay's hospital room – I couldn't look at my sick little boy; I just needed to remember him healthy and full of life. I remember not being able to get to the elevator fast enough and prayed that no one was inside. I don't recall if anyone was inside the elevator or walking out of the hospital. I was suddenly sitting on the curb crying. I needed to be alone - I didn't want to be consoled, or questioned, I needed to vent. I was furious and overwhelmed with emotions. I breathed, I sat and I thought about Clay. I envisioned him well, his smile and love of life. I knew what we had to do and went back upstairs and let Tim know that I thought we should proceed – his conclusion was the same. No matter what the outcome, we had to try.

It's ironic that when you are outside of the hospital the religion which you choose to believe is so important, but when your child's future is uncertain, I anyway –I welcomed any faith that could help my son. I learned that God was not necessarily one religion, but faith in itself and I welcomed prayers from anyone that wished to pray for Clay. He had a rabbi, priest and minister in his room praying for him – at separate times, of course. A Methodist prayer group knitted him a prayer shawl and I attended a non-denominational service in the chapel. Tim visited the Padre Pio shrine by our home and prayer groups of every faith had Clay on their list. I even massaged his head with holy water and holy oil, hoping that the seizures would subside and surgery could be avoided.

The morning of the surgery came and his condition remained the same. My parents and Tim's came to the hospital and we walked Clay down to surgery. I had a moment to tell my son a lifetime of feelings, but I knew that he had heard me for the past six weeks, so I simply gave him a kiss and told him how very much I loved him. Tim did the same and Clay was wheeled away. Now what were we supposed to do? We read every magazine and newspaper, made phone calls, watched television, had lunch, waited and mostly prayed. It got later and later and still no Clay. Finally, the doctor came out and informed us that the surgery went well. They were able to perform a ¾ corpus callosotomy and take a brain biopsy. They even wrapped his tiny head, so that I wouldn't have to see the stitches in the immediate future (I informed them in advance that I do not do well with my children's blood and they appeased me).

Most importantly, they implanted a grid within his head to get a more accurate assessment of seizure activity – it would remain for a couple of days and then be surgically removed. I really wasn't listening, I just wanted to see my son and know that he was alright.

Needless to say, I couldn't get to Clay's room fast enough and found him like the surgery had not ever occurred – except now his little head was completely bandaged. The technicians were hooking him up to the EEG machine; IV lines were being reattached and the soft hum of his ventilator filled the room again. All was well, except that I had become an expert at reading the EEG machine, and when it began monitoring Clay's brain activity there were seizures on both sides. I froze and knew exactly what this meant. We had elected to have our son endure brain surgery and it didn't work. The seizures were still on both sides of his brain and there was nothing more they could do for him. I became furious. I was angry at myself, the doctors, the situation and probably even God at that point. How could this be happening? Why was this happening? Tim and my mother told me to calm down. It had been a long day - maybe Clay's brain just needed to rest and have the added sedation wear off. We all knew that this was not the case. My mind was racing and recollecting everything that has transpired from the day's events. I was deflated and needed to shut down. Tim and I would have to talk to the doctors in the morning. I don't remember falling asleep that night, but at some point I finally did.

We met with the doctors, who let us know that the surgery went well. They were able to get a biopsy of Clay's brain and the inserted grid would monitor his activity for the following couple of days. I didn't bring up the fact that I could read the EEG machine and saw the seizures the previous evening. I was tired of thinking and analyzing. I needed a couple of days at this point to not research and just be a Mommy. So, I let Tim know that my wish was to forego our conversation with the team until they had results in their hands. One of Clay's doctors covered the EEG machine and placed a sign on it saying, "Do not look." He was joking, but probably a little serious (I had become an expert at reading the EEG machine – this was the only indication that I had Clay was "there" so I watched it constantly). I agreed half-heartedly, to stay away from it for a few of days. After all, they were the experts and we were just parents.

Three days later - we were ready. I was armed with

questions and my guard was up for what they were going to say to us. I feared the worst, but, when they entered the room I would have never fathomed what came next. After we had expressed our horror that the seizures had not subsided and were still radiating on both sides of Clay's brain, one of the doctors said, "What are your thoughts?" I remember thinking, "Excuse me? What are my thoughts? Isn't this your expertise?" Oh my (probably, a tame version of what I actually said) – they didn't know the answers!

A million thoughts raced through my head and I realized that Clayton's life was in our hands as much as the doctors. They weren't god – they didn't have the solutions. A magic crystal ball wasn't in their pocket. They had a degree and studied a different subject than Tim and I in school – we stood on the same ground. They ate the same food, probably watched some of the same programs and maybe even frequented establishments that our family visited. But, there was a very large difference – we stayed, while at the end of their shift, they went home. When their workday was done - ours continued. While they watched our son during rounds and read about him in report – we watched him 24 hours a day, as we had done since the day he was born.

This realization empowered me to fight, to have hope and, mostly, to take the reins of parenting my child again. I had a voice to express my opinions. I could say, "No,", "why "and "I don't agree." I learned at that moment that we were Clayton's greatest advocates. I was given a gift that day – I was given back my son.

A New Thought Process

Tim and I sat down in mid-December and assessed the situation. We had to be mutually on board with the direction of Clay's care. We left the hospital room that day and ate at an outside location. We decided from the beginning of Clay's hospital stay, that any discussion that could him alarm, would not be done in his room. A wonderful nurse told us that he had a patient awake from a coma and the child could recall conversations and voices. I did not want to take any chances of Clay hearing anything but positive reinforcement, so rounds and discussions, always took place in the hallway or a conference room. On that day, I wanted not only for Clay not to hear what we discussed, but I needed to not look at my son's face as we spoke. I had to remove myself as parent and look objectively at the situation.

Clay had now been in the hospital for two months. He underwent brain surgery, a brain biopsy, plasmapheresis, a G-tube placement and a tracheostomy. He was hooked up to a ventilator, EEG machine, multiple central and IV lines, a feeding pump and a monitor (heart rate, oxygen, CO_2, blood pressure). The medications took a toll on his organs and he developed pancreatitis, thrush, blood pressure issues and daily fluctuations on blood counts and organ functions. The hospital was essentially keeping Clay alive and his condition was not improving.

So, Tim and I talked. We weren't parents, or even husband and wife as we spoke – we were doctors with an honorary degree. We pointed out the obvious to each other and removed our feelings. I don't know how we did it, but we had no choice, we needed to come up with a solution. We went over the entire hospital stay, procedures and where this was all going to lead. Finally, we both realized that removing ourselves was not how Clay's situation would be solved. This was our son, our responsibility and the love of our lives. This little person who was fighting unbelievable odds – was still here. Tim and I sat down to come up with a solution, but this was not our problem to solve. We, as parents, were going to put our faith in our child and God. We would support him through each hurdle and let his body and spirit decide if it could get well. But, we were going to give him the opportunity. We were going to call the shots for our child and, hopefully, the doctors would agree. We were going to take him out of the coma and, ultimately, take him home.

We spoke with our families, mostly my parents and our children. The process of getting Clayton out of the coma was not going to be an easy task, as it was not able to be done to this point. Also, this process would not happen overnight – which meant that the time in the hospital would be lengthy. My parents agreed with our decision and my mother offered to extend her leave of absence to watch Ashley and Ashton. My mother was my rock. Many times, when I just needed to cry, she let me do so freely. I am sure being my mother - her heart was breaking, so she did the only thing that she could for me – she was there for my children and gave them a stable environment. Ashton, thankfully, was too young to understand anything other than he was being loved. Ashley was old enough to understand the severity of the situation. She could see that her brother was not improving and we talked to her openly about Clayton. Were we completely honest with her every step of the way? The answer would be, no. We felt that there was no need to worry her constantly and we wanted her to continue living her life. We let Tim's family know and my brother and our countless friends following Clayton's website.

Until this point, I have not mentioned one of the most

wonderful resources we were blessed with in the hospital, Clayton's

care page. The hospital offered a complimentary website to update

friends and family of your child's condition and progress. We

named Clayton's page, *Clayton the Great*, after a movie that Clay

and Tim watched before he got sick. The website was valuable

beyond words, literally. We would update friends and family daily

of his progress, the good and the bad, and wrote it as though Clayton

was writing the updates. Daily, we would receive wonderful words

of encouragement that we would print out and read to Clayton before

bed each evening (bedtime for us, unfortunately, Clayton just slept).

As the months progressed, so did Clayton's following. Word spread

through our network of family and friends and, ultimately, his page

had hundreds of viewers. Although these people weren't physically

there with us, their spirit helped us to get through some of the worst

moments. They also gave us the strength to face some of the biggest

challenges during his hospital stay.

So, we had the support and strength of so many individuals

praying and cheering our son on. We took a breath and asked to

meet with Clayton's medical team. One by one, which was many

doctors at this point, Tim and I let them know our thoughts. We wanted Clayton out the coma and we would deal with the seizures. Our son could not remain in the coma. Each day that passed, a little more of his brain functions were lost, so a game plan had to be put in place. We were aware of the consequences, but for the first time since this nightmare began, we felt like we were *doing* something. I am sure that the doctors' thoughts at this point must have been that we were letting go, but it couldn't have more to the contrary. We felt for the first time that we were going uphill; we were fighting, not daily watching our son slip away. Each doctor in every specialty agreed and maybe they thought otherwise, but they let us have hope that Clay would come out of this – never promising his condition once that happened.

I have to say, because I have not verbalized it up until this point, that we were blessed with an extraordinary team of medical professionals. We spoke and they listened. We yelled and lost our patience - they still listened. They cried with us, which I am sure is not a common practice in the medical profession, and offered comfort regularly. Tim and I were asked repeatedly about our family, not because it was going in a report, but because they wanted to know the little boy behind the illness. There were times, I am certain, that they thought we were blind to the outcome of the situation, but they never once shattered our hopes. Instead, we were allowed to join them in researching options and trials that could potentially stop the seizures. On more than one occasion, I had a doctor come into Clayton's room and sit down to watch a movie with me, or laugh with us at a show on the television. They became more than doctors to Tim and I, they became allies.

Getting Clayton's pentobarbital level reduced, which in turn would stop the coma, was not an easy task. As the medication was lowered, his heart rate would increase and the seizures would escalate. Tim and I would have to take shifts staying awake to chart each seizure because if they came too close to each other, he would go into status (a seizure that would not end on its own) and the pentobarbital would have to be increased. It was a vicious cycle that was not allowing the medication to be lowered. Then, we realized what was transpiring – he was going through withdrawal. The symptoms were evident and we let his medical team know our thoughts and findings. Then, one remarkable evening that turned the situation around, one of his evening nurses talked to the doctor about administering Fentanyl to reduce his anxiety from the withdrawal –

it worked! His heart rate lowered and he slept seizure free.

The next morning his team assembled and came up with a plan to combat the withdrawal and lower the Pentobarbital. The problem was that Pentobarbital is a barbiturate (a class of drugs) which, unfortunately, does not have a medication to combat its side effects. This did not stop Clayton's team from researching and finding a solution. They found a study in which Phenobarbital was utilized in high dosing to combat the side effects of the Pentobarbital wean. The risk was that the levels were extremely high, for anyone, let alone a 6-year-old boy. Tim and I agreed that the outcome outweighed the risk and we had to try this option. The team assembled, calculated, researched and came up with a game plan for the wean. It would take time, but we were all confident that the goal could be achieved, so we proceeded.

Around this time, our second miracle occurred during Clayton's hospital stay. Tim's brother and sister-in-law asked us if their priest could come and pray over Clayton. We agreed, of course, and welcomed his prayers especially during this time of uncertainty. He prayed over Clayton and let us know that every child has a guardian angel - also, that the angel would make its name evident, so that we could pray to it. I asked the priest, "How will I know the angel's name?" He replied, "You will know." I felt as though my brain could not absorb anything at that point, let alone know when a sign presented itself, but I accepted his response. We thanked him for coming and I forgot about the conversation until the next day.

I was in the family lounge area on the ICU floor and noticed a couple of drawings hanging on the wall. There was a sign posted letting the parents know, to please take a picture and hang in your child's room – they were gifts from local children. I thought that the sentiment was so sweet and selected a stick figure on blue construction paper. It had a round head, a little body, arms and legs and looked like it was probably drawn by someone of Clayton's age. I brought it back to the room and hung it directly above the head of his bed and explained the story to him. He had many drawings at this point that children from our community had made - in fact his walls were filled with get well posters and cards. This one, though, had such innocence and pulled at my heart. I wasn't sure why, but I felt the need to place it close to Clay.

I went down to get coffee and upon arriving back to the room

I was given a card from a local charity. While I was gone, Zoe (from Sesame Street) was making rounds on the floor and stopped in to have a photograph taken with Clayton. I did not allow any photographs of Clayton to be taken, up until this point, but I was not there to object – thankfully. They handed me the card and I thanked them for coming to visit. I didn't open it when they left. I didn't need to see Clayton hooked up to so many machines, nor did I wish to remember the sight after he was well, so I thumb tacked it to the wall with his other cards. Although, curiosity eventually got the best of me, and the next day I opened the card to view his photograph. Clayton, Zoe and the drawing at the head of Clayton's bed were staring back at me – I couldn't breathe, this time in pure awe. The stick figure was no longer in the photograph! An angel was on the blue construction paper. She had a white dress, wings and hair and the name on the bottom of the photograph was evident, "Caitlin." I seriously lost my breath for a moment as I was standing in the middle of a miracle.

I called Tim and my mom. I called in his nurses and word spread throughout the ICU. Nurses came in the room and gasped and even the doctors, who didn't believe before entering (and told me this later), were speechless. Those who were skeptical thought it was maybe the reflection of the flash in the photograph, but when they tried to recreate it, the image wasn't the same. Word of "Caitlin" spread throughout the hospital and we made sure that anyone who entered his room had the chance to view her. I never had so much faith, as I did the moment that I first saw her. I knew in my heart that Clayton would make it and there were powers greater than medicine that would aide in his recovery.

Caitlin was my sign that I could put faith into the unknown for my son's survival, but I received another equally important sign from Ashton that month. December was upon us and as the days progressed in the hospital, they also continued without us at home. Tim and I were leaving the hospital more than in the beginning to see the kids, but with Clayton's Phenobarbital wean we both had to split sleeping hours, so that he could be monitored for breakthrough seizures. He no longer had one-on-one nursing, which was an indication that his condition had improved, but it meant that one of us had to be awake at all times. So, at this point when we went home, it was not for an extended length of time, unless I had to work. I photographed weddings with my mother and, typically, she would drop me back at the hospital at the end of the evening. This particular evening, I chose to stay the night. It was a night both of heartache and enlightenment.

Friends of mine had been watching the kids on Tuesday evenings when my mom visited the hospital and helped my father when we had weddings to photograph. I was truly blessed by how many people helped my family so willingly. We stopped at my friend's house to pick up Ashton (Ashley had gone to a friend's house) and found him playing in the TV room behind a portable baby gate. He was having a wonderful time with my friend's daughter and became extremely excited when he saw us enter. I could not wait to hold my baby boy! My friend picked him up and walked over to give him to me and he started to cry. He wiggled to get out of my reach and into my mother's arms. I could tell by her expression that her heart broke for me, but I let her take him to the car with tears streaming down my face. My baby boy did not know or want me at that moment and I was devastated. I deserved it – I left him and Ashley. He didn't understand the situation or the reasoning. All that he knew was that my mother and father were there to console him, love him, and Tim and I were not. I was removed when I was home – I functioned, but I felt like I was in a fog. I loved my children more than life, but I was numb, because if I was numb this situation wouldn't hurt so terribly bad. Cloning was not an option, so I did the best that I could, but it obviously wasn't enough. My then nine month old hero taught me the greatest lesson I would learn. I needed to be a mommy again to all of my children. I needed to leave Clay and trust that Tim, the doctors and God would watch over him. He would be alright and I would be a much better Mommy for them all if I stepped back out into their world. I will always feel guilt, but I did what I felt was best at the time. I had to learn that it was alright to feel, live and enjoy my other children - even though my other son was clinging to life. Thank you, Ashton; I have no doubt that this is one of the reasons that God blessed us with you.

I could tell when I told Tim what had transpired, his heart broke for me. We both knew what had to happen and we agreed to split our time at the hospital, at least a couple of nights a week to start. It was the holidays and Ashley and Ashton deserved it to be a wonderful holiday season. We missed so much in 2 months and we needed to be in our children's lives again, not just present. Clay was not going to be coming home anytime soon, but we knew in our hearts that he would be home. This holiday we would get through and with the help of our family and friends we would enjoy through the heartache.

Our township dedicated the Christmas tree lighting ceremony to Clayton and once again raised donations to help with our everyday expenses. I was continually touched at the outpouring of support and compassion shown to our family by so many, those we knew and those who we had never met. A friend of mine put in a request at her job and the kids were visited by Marines and Santa (carrying gifts) through the wonderful organization, "Toys for Tots." I was able to use the donations from the construction workers at the hospital and various donations to shop for Christmas presents for the kids that they put on Santa's list and a little tree for Clayton's hospital room. There was such an outpouring of support, but I needed to go to a store and shop. I had to continue the Christmas shopping tradition. I needed to bring my list and shop for all three of our children and have some normalcy. Ashley, my mom and I shopped that year – I even bought Clay a chess set that he always wanted. Most, importantly, I smiled. I didn't need to think about it, or feel guilty that I was doing it – I just smiled because I was happy.

Tim and I decided that I would go home Christmas Eve and we would switch at midnight. That plan would allow me to read Christmas bedtime stories to all 3 kids and enjoy Christmas Eve dinner with Ashley, Ashton and my parents. Tim would be there to open presents, but I could tuck them in. My mother, with such love, let me know that she and my father would bring Christmas Dinner (including China and silver) to the hospital; therefore, we could all eat together. The plan was set.

I left the hospital Christmas Eve afternoon and cried the entire ride home. I loved Christmas. I loved the traditions that we made as a family, the look in my children's eyes and the countdown to the big day. This year was so different, but I would try to enjoy where I was in the present and live in the present. I did just that – I pulled up to the house, opened the door and heard the wonderful commotion of my children. We ordered Chinese (another family Christmas tradition); I touched base with Tim and enjoyed the evening. Someone was missing, but Tim wasn't there either, so it wasn't just one chair missing from the table (that aspect made Clay's absence a little easier). A community contacted my mother about

71

dropping off gifts to the kids (they select a family each year and read about us in the paper) and I was fortunate to be home when they arrived Christmas Eve. The woman told me how sorry she was and I walked out of the room and cried, but I didn't continue to do so. I took a breath, walked back out and hugged her. This wonderful person, who we had never met, just presented such a kind gesture to us on Christmas Eve – I was going to let myself enjoy the happiness of this moment and not feel guilty.

We let Ashley and Ashton open one big gift on Christmas Eve that year. This would give me the opportunity to see their faces, since I would be at the hospital Christmas morning. Ashley loved her present (a video camera) and Ashton was thrilled at just ripping the paper. I got them ready for bed and snuggled between them. I felt heartache and joy at the same moment. We read Christmas stories and I just held them. I wanted time to stop. Tim and I agreed to this, but I wanted to see them open their presents. At the same time, I wanted to read Clayton's Christmas stories to him – this was agony. I never realized how many times your heart can break; it seemed like a daily occurrence. I gave them a kiss, told them how much I loved them and told them to call me in the morning after they opened their gifts. I felt as though I was having visitation with my children again, but I was trying to make the situation seem very normal.

Back at the hospital, I wished Tim a Merry Christmas and he left for home. I stood there in Clay's room and felt very much alone. There was no music, or lights (we weren't allowed to plug in his tree) and his presents under the tree would not be opened by him this year. I looked over at him, lying there, and then I realized how magical of a Christmas it truly was – he was here for Christmas. He beat all of the odds and was here. I was able to be with Ashley and Ashton and would be Christmas Day. Tim and I navigated the arrangements, along with the help of my parents, and we made it work. I grabbed his book and started to read him a Christmas story – this is what is Christmas was all about, family. I fell asleep next to Clay that night reading him his stories and dreamed of my two children at home.

Christmas morning was quiet. I tried to pretend it was just another day and not wonder what was happening at home; although, I could think of nothing else that morning. I talked to the kids on the phone, counted the minutes until they arrived and welcomed the commotion once everyone did. My parents (arms full of presents and coolers full of food) arrived with the kids and Tim. We opened presents, including Clayton's and the hospital room dissolved. It was Christmas and we were celebrating as a happy family, not a family in the ICU of a hospital. I helped my mother and father set up Christmas dinner in the playroom down the hall (there wasn't enough room in Clay's room) and she invited other parents in the ICU to make a plate for themselves. We went back and forth to Clay's room and enjoyed every moment.

I had a different outlook after going through the Christmas season. I was given miracles, both of the spiritual and physical worlds and intended to use the lessons that I was shown. I knew that there were no guarantees, but at that moment I was happy and I wasn't going to think about tomorrow. When Ashley, Ashton and my parents left that night, I cried, as usual. It hurt terribly to wave goodbye to the kids, but I knew in my heart that we could be a family no matter what the circumstances. I would no longer let guilt and fears dictate my choices – it was alright to smile, laugh and enjoy life, even if one of my children was in the hospital.

The Uphill Climb

The New Year brought new possibilities, outlooks and a building excitement for the future. Clayton's medical team came up with a formal Phenobarbital wean schedule, which meant that the medication would be completely weaned by the end of January. The medical team, I am sure thought that we had finally lost our minds, when Tim and I put a large calendar on the outside of his door marked (in large letters), Phenobarbital wean countdown. Each day we marked a big red X on the number and continued the countdown. As the medication was lowered we saw his body gradually renew itself. One by one the countless medications were discontinued and, with each order removed, an IV line was removed from his body. His organ function continued to daily improve and, even seizures, were remaining under control.

When his EEG lines were finally removed, one of his nurses gave him a much needed hair wash and cut. On another occasion one of his nurses, literally said, "Enough is enough – he does not need this anymore." She proceeded to remove his rectal thermometer (that was continuously inserted), took him off of the cooling pad (regulating his body temperature) and dressed him in hospital pajamas. The nurses called these acts of kindness; Claytons "much needed spa treatments." My heart melted at their compassion and perseverance to make him whole again.

Tim and I split our days, so that each of us was home three days consecutively with Ashley and Ashton and we both stayed up at the hospital on Sundays. This plan, of course, was a perfect scenario until Clayton would "misbehave," which typically meant that we were both back at the hospital. We tried to juggle as much as we were able, now knowing that Clayton was stable. When I was home, I tried to spend more time in our house, rather than constantly remaining at my parents. Our home was beginning to feel normal again, or maybe just I was beginning to feel normal. Tim and I, though, were literally seeing each other on Sundays and speaking on the phone. We would walk each other downstairs, when we changed "shifts," but each of us was alone with Clayton. I had no doubt that we were confident in his care, at least of what we had learned up to that point, though, it was still frightening at times to be solely in the decision making process. We adapted and had increased confidence in our abilities.

I bumped into one of Clayton's doctors (a toxicologist and head of the ER) in the lobby one day in January and he stopped to talk to me. He was a wonderful man and his experience and knowledge Tim and I both came to admire and respect. As a person, his personality and compassion put us at ease – on more than one occasion. On this day, he asked if he could come up to Claytons room to speak to Tim and I. Of course I agreed and after exchanging pleasantries, he pulled out his calendar (smart phones were not utilized in 2005) and asked Tim and I to do the same. He sat us down and told us, not asked us, that we were going out to dinner and he was going to "babysit." We were speechless and if he were not so insistent, we never would have gone. I felt guilty leaving the hospital to enjoy an evening out, when if I was leaving; I should be going home to the kids. I also felt extremely guilty going out to enjoy myself, while so much was happening in our lives. I must say, though, it was exactly what Tim and I needed. We went to a restaurant down the street from the hospital and enjoyed a wonderful meal, compliments of a gift card given to us by another doctor for Christmas, and we actually talked about home. We walked and talked on the way back to the hospital and even stopped to sit on a park bench to extend this hiatus. I didn't let myself feel guilty – I let myself enjoy an evening with my husband.

Tim's and my relationship was definitely strained at times during Clay's hospital stay, as any marriage would be in our situation. I do not want to make it seem as though Tim and I constantly agreed and were loving towards each other. We both have extremely strong personalities and like to be in control of the situation – that does not always work well when you need to be united for medical decisions. We learned to appreciate each other and mostly, appreciate that the other had a valid opinion. On some days that worked and on others, we would go outside and say exactly what we needed to express. Prior to Clayton's illness, we had the typical marriage of "bumping into each other in the hallway." due to Tim's work schedule. Now, in the hospital, we spent 24 hours a day (seven days a week) in the same hospital room for countless days and nights. I told Tim at one point that I knew exactly why the windows in the hospital did not open – either we would have pushed each other out or jumped at some point. Obviously, that was said in jest. Characteristics we were least fond of in ourselves; lack of patience and the need to control – were magnified daily. In time we learned to subdue our emotions when it was warranted or leave them room to compose ourselves. Ultimately, we learned that when we argued we usually weren't even mad at something the other did –

just the situation that we had no control over and, in turn, we were

taking it out on each other. We learned more about each other

during those months, than we ever knew in all of the years that we

had been married. We learned to work together towards a goal of

going home as a family.

The month of January was all about just that – family. All of

us, Tim's and my family, the kids and our friends eagerly watched as

Clayton's Pentobarbital wean was coming to an end. This

nightmare, it seemed would soon be over, so we began to make

preparations for the upcoming event. My mother and I talked about

ordering a cake for the day that wean stopped and we knew exactly

the style – Spiderman, Clayton's favorite superhero. The

supermarket, I am sure, never took an order for such wording on a

cake, "0 Pentobarbital"; it would read in large red letters. On an

unforgettable day in January, the cake was delivered by my parents

and children, and the Pentobarbital was turned off. The IV line

administering the medication was disconnected and his nurse eagerly

removed the machine from his room. We hugged, cried and mostly

savored the moment. Clayton was still not awake; we were hoping due to the heavy dosing of Phenobarbital, so we gathered next to his bed and enjoyed the moment. Family brought balloons and even the medical staff on the floor came in to celebrate. We were not thinking about the future, we were living in the present, and going forward.

The doctors began to ask us regularly if we saw any indication of him waking up – to which Tim and I replied, "Should he be?" It never crossed our minds that he wouldn't wake up after being taken out of the coma and we didn't visit that possibility. I did not have "hope" of his improvement because that meant there was a chance that he would not improve; I knew he would come back to us. He did just that, days later. I glanced over one afternoon and thought that I saw Clay move his finger, but dismissed the notion as wishful thinking. After a couple of minutes, he not only slightly moved his finger, but ever so slightly opened his eyes. I cringed and waited for a seizure to appear (the only time we saw Clayton's eyes open was during a seizure), but his mouth did not move (the other facial indication of his seizures). He closed his eyes and opened them again, before going back to sleep. I can only compare this feeling to the day he was born and I looked down at him for the first time. I was in awe of my son and a huge lump formed in my throat. I called Tim to let him know and he didn't need to say a word, his voice and silence spoke volumes. He let me know that he thought he saw something the previous day, but didn't want to unwarrantedly get my hopes up, so he kept it to himself. I, then, called my mother and Ashley and ran to update his Care page – I couldn't type fast enough. I knew that we had a long road ahead, but Clayton beat the odds and that would be my focus. I smiled thinking about his future, for the first time since we arrived at the hospital. I didn't have to force a smile, or think about doing so, and I cried tears of joy. This day was his second birthday, the day we were blessed with him again. I slept that night, through the night, for the first time in a very long time. When I awoke in the morning, I smiled and knew that this was the first day on our road to going home. I could plan for future events again and know that Clay would be present in our lives.

We planned Ashton's 1st birthday for the end of the month. I elected to hold it at a local baby gym and he had a ball. All of our family and close friends attended the celebration for my little man. It was normal again for him to reach up for me to hold him – but, I never took it for granted. We were blessed again at the end of the party when the facility would not let me pay. They told me that they saw our name on the sheet and read about Clayton's story in the newspaper – they were donating to our family. I was speechless. At that moment, I realized that Clayton was making a difference in people's lives and bringing out the compassion of strangers. I looked over and saw Ashton smiling, Ashley laughing, Tim talking with friends and my parents standing together amongst a crowd of family – life at this moment was perfect. Clay was not present, but he was, he was just in another location. He was where he needed to be and so were we.

I knew the progress with Clay would be steady, but slow. That being said, I tried to be involved in as many aspects of home life that was possible. I refused to miss any more milestones of my children's lives, so I came up with ways that would allow me to be in two places at a time. Sometimes this plan would work better than others; one in particular was extremely successful. Ashley was in a wonderful Girl Scout troop and over the months I was not able to attend many of her functions. I felt horrible, as her cookie sale was approaching (a big deal in the world of Girl Scouts) and to let her fail because I was unable to man a booth, was not an option. I sat down with her and let her know that Clayton and I would help her sell more cookies than she could imagine. She helped me to set up a stand which rested against Clayton's hospital room door. We stacked the boxes and hung a large sign on top of the pile which said, "I am selling cookies for my sister. Please leave your money in the can. Love, Clayton." Did the plan work? Ashley sold seven *cases* of cookies through Clayton's stand that year. Parents, siblings of patients and medical personnel all stopped to purchase cookies. Word spread through the hospital and people from other floors and departments came up and purchased boxes – even in the middle of the night, I would hear the money being left in the can. I was elated that the plan worked and, most importantly, Ashley was happy. She sold more cookies that year than anyone in her troop. Equally important, the hospital staff said nothing to waiver her sales; instead, they cheered her on for her accomplishments.

Clayton was steadily making accomplishments of his own. He was now awake most of the day. He was able to move his arms and legs to get away from the nurses. Obviously, they were so pleased to see him respond that they antagonized him (lovingly) to make him respond more. Only one IV line remained and this was being left in the event that an emergency medication was needed for seizure relief. His muscles were weak and PT/OT was regularly visiting him and teaching us strategies for his improvement. We were learning, as was he, for we had no idea much was lost due to previous constant seizures. Clayton could not hold his head up, eat, talk, walk or follow many commands. His neurological level was that of an infant and his prognosis was still uncertain. We didn't let that stop us from pushing, as we were now his voice. That persistence is how we were introduced to a new therapy and a wonderful woman.

Clay had been on every seizure medication available in the United States – with no success. We still read about options; although, we were certain that medication was not an option to control his seizures. That is when we were introduced to the Ketogenic Diet program. This was a holistic approach to seizure control. Instead of a medication to quiet his brain, the diet was successful in some patients at minimizing (sometimes eliminating) seizure activity. It was worth a try. I felt that this option was the least invasive therapy that we had tried since Clayton's seizures began and I completely trusted the woman who ran the program. I met and spoke with not only parents, but children within the program. They were remarkable and not patients within the hospital, they were home with their families – I remember thinking, how quickly can we start?

The problem with Clayton's case was that many of the medications that were being administered to him would hamper the effectiveness of the diet. He was not eating by mouth, so the diet would consist of his formula and not food; therefore, a special formula had to been calculated. With much anticipation, the diet was started. I am not sure if it worked because so many medicines could have made the seizures subside, but something did – Clayton's seizures stopped. After over three months, there was not a single seizure visible. Neurologists on service could not believe this information when we brought it up to them in rounds. Maybe he was having subclinical seizures (not visible) that were not evident? They hooked Clayton back up to the EEG machine expecting to find seizure activity and none was present. We were told that Clayton's seizure activity could have run its course and those areas may no longer be functioning. No evidence was available to confirm or deny this notion. All I knew at that point was that we were one step closer to going home.

A week later, as Clayton was sitting in his wheelchair, his primary ICU doctor entered the room. He followed and coordinated Clayton's care since the first day. On many occasions he made us laugh with humor, but on this day he looked very serious. He asked me how Clayton was doing and I told the doctor that he was beginning to follow some simple commands. He looked at me questioningly. Tim was sitting next to me and what happened next left us both speechless. The doctor walked in front of Clay and said, "Hello Clayton," of course, Clayton did not respond. He then put his hand up and said, "Can you make the Vulcan sign for me?" I know that his doctor was not expecting Clayton to respond, but he did. Everyone in the room gasped, Clayton slowly raised his hand, separated his fingers and made the sign. His doctor looked at me, I could tell holding back emotion, and smiled. He gave Clayton a high five and his nurses hugged him. He told me later that he would watch Clayton and I through the window of his room and he had no doubt that Clayton could understand me.

The last IV line was removed the next day, which meant that

he would now be transferred to the step down Unit for continued rehabilitation and our teachings. We still did not have a set date, but this was the next step before being discharged to home. Home – I wouldn't let myself even go that far into the future. I knew that Clayton would get there, but I was still worried that if I got too excited something horrible would happen. We had been on a rollercoaster with his illness for so long, that the reality of "home" was put in the back of my mind. I was elated that he was being transferred and I waited for this for months. Why then, was I so sad?

We packed up everything that was accumulated since October. Some of the items we took home, while others were being sent to his new room. Nurses and doctors that cared for him in the ICU stopped in on the day of transfer and wished him well. I went into the bathroom, while Tim and team got Clayton ready to move and I cried. I was scared, emotionally drained and leaving the bubble of the ICU. These people were our lifeline and now they would be gone. This room held so many memories that all seemed to be hitting me at once and I felt as though we were leaving a part of Clayton in it. I had to leave this behind and start a ne new chapter in his life, so I took a hold of Clay's wheelchair and away we went.

Going Home

The step down Unit was very different than the ICU, but it was meant to be different. The concept was for parents to learn the equipment, their child's care and the daily routine, which we be administered at home. We met new doctors and nurses and I felt very much like when Clayton was first admitted. His room was in a different area of the hospital, so even the elevators and route to the unit were unfamiliar. I missed the usual faces that I would see daily and mostly, the relationships that had been formed with these people. During the initial stages of Clayton's hospital stay, Tim was there with me, so I was comforted when I was "homesick." Now, Tim was home when I was with Clay and I felt very much alone. I know now that this was part of the goal of the hospital, as well as rehabilitation. Obviously, they do not want parents to get too comfortable with their surroundings, so as to not want to leave. This was not my thought process, by any means; I just wanted familiarity to get me through this next phase with Clayton. I hung his pictures and decorated his room. Finally, it looked more "kid like" and not as sterile – it was an improvement.

Clayton was on a very rigorous weaning schedule. The hope

was that many of the medications which remained would be discontinued prior to discharge. He was a trooper and continued to beat the odds. Tim and I oversaw the schedule and met with the team daily to outline his goals and progress. He was making unbelievable progress in Physical Therapy and began crawling with support. His muscles were strengthening, as well, and he would listen when I read him his favorite books at night. He even started to watch television. He had swallow studies to see if he was able to eat and during one of these it was discovered that both his tonsils and adenoids were extremely large for his airway. He was scheduled for a Tonsillectomy/adenoidectomy with the hope that a possible decannulation (removal of the tracheal tube) could take place prior to going home. This was unbelievable news and we signed the papers, feeling that this was Clayton's best chance for a full respiratory recovery.

Meanwhile at home, plans were forming for Clayton's homecoming. We needed to make the house handicap accessible, so multiple interviews were set up with contractors. Two ramps would need to be installed, insuring that Clayton would have a primary and emergency exit route from the house. The kids' bathtub needed to be removed and a handicap shower stall installed, allowing Clayton access with his wheelchair. The carpeting in the bedrooms needed to be replaced, to reduce the amount of dander and dust. A new French door would need to replace our backdoor, allowing Clayton's wheelchair to fit through the doorway. The list seemed to grow each time that we sat down with the hospital and contractors. I don't know where we would be without our friends and family, as it was their compassion that allowed the renovations to take place. Friends and family gathered at a fundraiser held for Clayton's birthday and, once again, we were blessed with the outpouring of support. Due to the generous donations from this and other fundraisers, he would have everything that he needed to get well – his family, love, support and a home that would fit his new needs. The renovations began and we were given a date at the end of March for completion. We were all elated, until Clayton's surgery.

Tim and I met at the hospital the morning of his tonsillectomy. Clayton had so many procedures by this point, that it seemed routine to have our son wheeled to surgery; although, things never went according to plan with him. It also never got easier saying goodbye and counting the minutes until I would see him again. I was worried about this surgery, though, because I thought I saw a small seizure that morning. I wasn't positive and it didn't happen again. Tim and I let the doctors know and we all chose to proceed. The procedure was short and the doctor informed us that all went well. Clayton was still asleep in recovery when we went into the room, but when he opened his eyes we were horrified. His one pupil was dilated, while the other was "pinpoint." We called the nurses and doctors over and they didn't seem overly concerned – they attributed it to the sedation. From that point, the night went downhill. Clayton began to seize, probably due to the pain, so Ativan and Morphine had to be administered. He threw up blood, from his mouth and tracheal tube throughout the night (due to the surgery). By morning I, as well as his walls, were stained with blood. Tim and I were furious, scared and had not slept when his doctor did rounds in the morning. So, needless to say it was not a quiet conversation and the outcome was that Clayton was going back to the PICU. We did not blame the doctors or the nurses for that night. It was not their fault that Clayton did not follow the path of so many having this surgery. On the other hand, we had already seen what seizures could do to our son, and we were not waiting another 5 months for them to subside. We would live with the seizures. He was going home.

The next morning, we told the doctors all of the above. Clayton was going home March 23, 2005. That gave his medical team three weeks to do what they had to do and for us the same. Obviously, we were educated enough at this point to know that if he was not medically stable to go home, we nor the team would allow him to do so. We all proceeded. I called my mother and Ashley to tell them the news and Tim did the same with his parents – we were all going home.

Now, we scrambled. Three weeks seemed like an eternity until we realized just how much had to be done at home and in the hospital. We completed our training for Clayton's G-tube (to feed him), ventilator and learned CPR. Interviews took place with nursing companies and I remember thinking, what in the world was I supposed to know about hiring a nursing company? Tim liked the clinical approach to home nursing, while I wanted "warm and fuzzy" personalities to take care of our son. We talked, debated and chose a company that would provide both our nurses and equipment. Ease of access, is exactly what I needed at that point in my life.

94

Time flew, and before I knew it, it was the day before discharge. We spoke to the nursing company and they arranged to have Clayton's new nurses meet us at the house. The construction was almost complete; a cleaning crew came in to sanitize the house, medial equipment was delivered and Clayton's room was transformed into a mini ICU. My mother and I went food shopping to stock the barren cabinets and refrigerator and, finally, we picked up Clayton's medications. We were done. The house was ready for a family again. My parents drove me up to the hospital that night. I would ride in the ambulance with Clay the next day and Tim would drive home in our car. We were ready, I knew that we were – but, I did not a sleep at all that night. Going home was nothing short of surreal. I imagined, during Clayton's worst moments, this day. I knew that it would come and never let myself think otherwise. But, now I was not imagining. We were finally going home. We were all getting our lives back with Clay beside us.

March 23, 2005 arrived. I remember that Tim went down to get me coffee; although, my emotions were so high, that caffeine was not needed, but welcomed. We completed countless pieces of paperwork and I, anyway half listened to directions. My mind was already somewhere else and I couldn't get there fast enough. The transport team arrived and assembled Clayton, with Caitlin's photograph beside him, onto the stretcher. I walked out of the room first and looked up to find his nurse, from the very first night, standing in the doorway. This man, who had made such a difference in our world, was there to say goodbye. I hugged him and thanked him for everything that he had done for Clayton and our family. No words would ever adequately express my gratitude. We cried together many times previously – this time, was no exception. As I turned to leave he said something that I will never forget, "Now, go take your son home." We did just that – we followed the hallways to the ambulance. Along the way, we seemed to pass countless people that we knew, and I felt as though Clayton was a dignitary on a parade route. He was hugged and there were plenty of tears – this time of happiness.

The ride home was even more surreal than the previous evening and when the ambulance pulled into our driveway, I didn't lose a moment in jumping out. My mother had the kids out on the porch and I rushed to scoop them up into my arms. Tears of joy streamed down my face and I said to my mom, "we're home." I walked into my house; full of people to get Clayton situated in his room, and just took it all in. I hadn't walked into my house in over five months, knowing that all of my children were with me under one roof. I must have walked by Clayton's room a dozen times that day just to make sure that I wasn't dreaming – I wasn't, he was home.

The first evening home though, wasn't completely without heartache. I guess I thought that when we walked through the door our lives would magically resume. We would be a family again and pick up as though five months didn't happen. Ashley and Ashton were now used to a new set of routines and my parent's house was the home that they knew. I didn't think that Ashton wouldn't remember our life before this nightmare, but he made it evident at dinner. I put Ashton in his highchair and we sat down to eat. My mother went to her house and Ashton started to cry – an extremely sad cry. I tried to console him and my heart broke. To him, this was not home, so as much as it tore me apart, I picked him up and brought him over to my parents. The same things occurred when I tried to put him to bed in his crib. I called my mother over to console him – her comfort is what put him to sleep. She cried when she left that evening and my heart broke for her. We were rebuilding lives and she probably felt as though she was losing our children. They had become her life for five months and I am sure that it broke her heart to go home without them. Thankfully, only a door now separated the two houses (and lives). This would take time, not an aspect that I ever realized, nor let myself consider. But, we were home and we would have 24 hours a day to help Ashley and Ashton adjust. We would all have to adjust.

Ashley was in the television room, when I walked out of my bedroom, and she asked if she could lay down with Clay. Of course, I was elated at her question and welcomed a little glimpse of the past. She grabbed a book, moved the countless wires (with the help of Clayton's nurse in the room) and laid down next to her brother. He tilted his head towards her and I ran to get the camera. I didn't want to forget this moment and I needed to have this memory to view for whatever challenges were ahead. I called for Tim and my mother and we all peaked in on my daughter, far more mature than her years. Her "Clayton" was home and she was comforting him like she had done so many other nights before he got sick. I would have this memory now of his room and bed and no longer the haunting ones of the night he got sick.

I slept in my bed that night, next to my husband, for the first time in five months - we were home with our children, and tomorrow, we didn't have to go back to the hospital. I couldn't wait to wake up in the morning and know that this was not a dream.

The first morning and, those after, brought daily routines that I had not been a part of in months; from adjusting my sleep schedule to caring for Ashley and Ashton's needs. I had to reestablish a schedule within our home and acclimate my children to not only us being full time parents, but a nurse residing within their home for 16 hours a day. These changes did not happen overnight, nor did I learn, could I make them. The dream I had of stepping into the life that Tim and I built over the past 12 years, was just that, a dream. It served the purpose while we were in the hospital. Envisioning our life and reaching towards it gave me the strength to get through some of the worst times with Clayton. Though, the family that I remember, no longer existed. It tore me apart to be within our home and the memories were no longer a reality.

Clayton was slowly making progress. He was now only on the ventilator at night and even then, it was only to give him extra support. I don't know if he knew he was home, or remember that this was his home. I tried to keep his room exactly as it was prior to the hospital, just adding countless machines and supplies. Before getting sick, his prized possession was his bunk bed and I wouldn't waiver on having that removed. He and Ashley spent countless nights laughing and talking in his room – he on the bottom bunk and her being on the top. I would read stories to them at night in that bed and it was the bed that last held him healthy. For these reasons, I wouldn't let the medical company bring a hospital bed into his room. I wanted normalcy, even though I should have realized that a bunk bed and nursing functions would not work. After the first night, I was told that on more than one occasion the nurse bumped her head on the top bunk trying to situate Clayton. The following day we took off the top bunk, but his bottom bed remained in the room. After the first week, we were informed that the nurses were unable to position Clayton as they needed to during the night, so the medical company brought in a hospital bed. I cried when Tim and I brought the bed into the basement. I began to see how different my son and his needs were now, but I tried to keep as many things as possible as they were before he got sick. The problem was he was

100

not the same little boy.

His best friend, since Clayton was 3-years-old, visited him a number of times. Thankfully, his mother was (and is still) a dear friend of mine; otherwise, her son may not have known the "different Clayton" that he would encounter. This special little boy, sat right down next to Clay, and Clay leaned his head over towards his friend. Tears filled our eyes as we watched the innocence and friendship of two little boys – which sickness could not separate. Whatever emotions he was feeling, he never let it show. He talked to Clay like he had always done and, although Clay couldn't respond, he kept on talking. This child will always hold a place in my heart. We soon learned, however, that adults did not mask their emotions as well as children.

Tim and I decided to take all of our children to the zoo when the weather broke. It was a gorgeous day and we were so excited to be out as a family. This was the first family outing since Clay arrived home and we were in much need of a hiatus. Unfortunately, the day did not go as planned. We wheeled Clayton through the zoo, with his multiple pieces of medical equipment in a basket behind us. I pushed Ashton in his stroller and Ashley walked along side of me.

As we walked, people stopped and stared at Clayton. They looked at us and actually stopped. Ashley was aware of the onlookers and became uncomfortable, as did Tim and I. We felt as though we were on a parade route and I couldn't wait to leave. Then, a miracle happened. We passed a couple pushing their son in a wheelchair. They smiled and stopped to talk to us. Our day changed dramatically, as they spoke to Clay and asked us how we were enjoying our day. These strangers performed such a simple act of kindness and, in doing so, allowed us to enjoy the rest of the afternoon. Looking back, we were meant to meet them. I learned that people are typically curious and many times stare without the knowledge that they are doing so. Still, on many occasions after that day, I wished that I could have hung a sign on Clayton's wheelchair for the world to see. It would have simply read, "I was just like you and I still am on the inside."

I learned to live for the "good days" and struggled through the days full of seizures and medications. I enjoyed every moment with Ashley and Ashton – our lives were finally finding a new normalcy. Although, I had days that it took all of my power to get out of bed. I was depressed, but hid it well. I was no longer "functioning" as in the hospital; I was now feeling every emotion and it hurt. I was full of guilt, now being able to partake in Ashley and Ashton's milestones – it was never more evident how much I had missed. My heart broke watching Clayton struggle to perform the simplest of tasks and I missed being his "Mommy," instead of his nurse. Mostly – I missed "Clayton." The photographs on our walls showed a smiling, healthy little boy. His artwork still hung on the refrigerator and his book bag was still by the front door, but that child was no longer with us. I missed him terribly. I missed hearing his voice and seeing his smile. I wanted to hear him say, "Hold me" and "I love you." I wanted my child back. I wanted to give him the sleepover that he never had and walk on the beach. I would watch him sleeping and pretend that he would awake whole again, just to get through the agonizing moments. I was grieving, but felt guilt about that because he was still with us. I hoped in the beginning that he remembered his life, but as time went on – I wished for the opposite. I didn't want to think that he was trapped in his body and was unable to let us know.

I was tired of being strong and increasingly losing patience with other new aspects of our life. As much as we needed nursing in our home and valued their care for Clayton, I didn't want them there at times. We didn't have privacy and I felt as though I had to watch what I said to Tim and the kids. Though, when a nurse called out due to illness, I was upset that they weren't in our home. Clayton's medication schedule was every two hours (24 hours a day), which meant that either Tim or I did not sleep, if we didn't having nursing to help us. I was angry that I needed help and angry that I relied on their support. I wanted to control of my life and so many aspects were out of control – I was drowning. There was not a support group or book on a topic such as we experienced and no one completely understood what we were going through. Then, one day, I hopped on the computer and found exactly what I needed.

Clayton's diagnosis, due to multiple seizures, was Epilepsy. So, I reached out to the Epilepsy website and located a Parent to Parent chat group. The website, as well as the wonderful mothers whom I met – became my lifeline. I went online when I needed their support, advice and companionship (from those with a similar life as mine). Although I was blessed to have such a strong support system with Tim, my mother and friends, it was wonderful to have support through an outside source. When I felt as though I was drowning, I knew that these women had already made it through the situation. Sometimes, that made all of the difference in a day.

Coming home from the hospital brought as much pain as joy. It was a journey for our entire family that I did not anticipate. I realized that my periods of anger, grief, elation and dismay were all necessary parts of healing. Releasing my emotions made me a better parent, wife, daughter and person. I allowed myself to feel emotions as they happened and stopped feeling guilty for feeling such emotions. Our child was home, as were we with Ashley and Ashton. As the weeks turned into months, we became whole again and new memories replaced the sadness. Our family had made it through the most impossible of situations – together. The rest of our lives were ahead of us and we had the support, tools and strength (now) to make it through anything.

Life Goes On

Weeks turned into months and we saw a steady increase in Clayton's progress. We taught him how to throw a ball and hit a balloon tied to his wheelchair. If I held him upright, he would now try to take steps. Physical therapy, Occupational therapy and Speech teachers were coming to our home and teaching us, as well as Clayton, exercises to help strengthen his weakened muscles. Ashley and Ashton even joined in on the fun by frequently having a catch with Clayton. I no longer gauged his progress by what he still had to acquire, but more so, I marveled at the new tasks he was able to learn.

We took our annual vacation to the beach his first summer home. Why wouldn't we? I was determined to allow Clayton the opportunity to experience life – and this beach was our tradition since the kids were born. I was ready for this and visually pictured this place on days when I needed to escape. The beach was (is) my happy place. Once I cross the bridge, stress melts away. I love the sights, smells and sand between my toes. In fact, at one point in the hospital, I told a doctor that is exactly what Clayton needed – his feet in the sand. We did just that the first year back to the beach.

Clayton was wheeled to the beach in a beach buggy wheelchair, he was quite the hit of the beach, and we walked him straight down to the ocean. I picked him up, placed him on my lap and closed my eyes. Life was perfect. My mother, Tim and Clayton's nurse and I cried – tears of happiness. Clayton and Ashton seemed to enjoy the beach that year together (ironically they marveled at the same things). Sea gulls, beach umbrellas and the planes flying over offered hours of enjoyment – they both would sit and gaze in amazement at them all. I cried on my way to the beach that year, but smiled on the way home.

Unfortunately, our happiness was cut short a few weeks later. Clayton had a two hour seizure, which led to a hospital admission and a diagnosis of Viral Meningitis. I recall thinking, "Meningitis – really? How much can my child endure?" He was a trooper though and once again, beat the odds and came home 10 days later. The meningitis, though, brought back his seizures and started a vicious cycle. By the end of November, Clayton was readmitted to the hospital, with seizures so severe that another coma was introduced to us. Tim and I were devastated and refused. We would not allow Clayton to possibly lose everything that he fought so hard to regain.

We were not going back to the beginning almost exactly a year later - they would have to come up with a different plan this time. That is when another surgery took place and a VNS was placed within Clayton.

The purpose of the VNS was to stop a seizure as it began, by "learning" Clayton's brain activity. The device would send an electrical current at designated intervals 24 hours day and in addition, we were able to manually send a current when we saw a seizure. I thought that the hand held device was somewhat of placebo, as I did not feel it stopped a seizure while it was occurring. Although, the currents sent in automatic intervals allowed him to never go into status again.

December we were still in the hospital. Tim had started a new job, so he was not able to spend time in the hospital and I would not leave Clayton alone. Once again, my parents stepped up and watched Ashley and Ashton. I did the kid's shopping online that year, decorated our house for the holidays and most importantly, did not decorate Clayton's hospital room. We were on "home mode" now and no longer did I have the patience or heart for long hospital stays. I refused to spend another holiday in the hospital, or have

Clayton not be a part of his first Christmas home. Clayton needed to be with his family. In my exact words, I told one of his doctors, "I don't care if it takes Santa landing on the hospital roof to get him home. Clayton will make it home for Christmas this year." He was discharged December 23rd and was home with us for Christmas. In fact, Clayton never spent another birthday or holiday as a patient in the hospital.

Time progressed, and until we were blessed by another miracle, Clayton's progress declined. Tim and I received a call from Clayton's neurologist, asking us if we would be willing to speak to another family in our situation. The similarities of our children's stories were eerie, for lack of better words. They were both sick with a virus; presented with intractable seizures, they were the same age and this child was now in a Pentobarbital coma. We formed a friendship with this family that continues to this day. We spoke at length about our experiences and when Clayton was admitted for uncontrollable seizures, their son was still a patient in the hospital. It was them, this time, that offered support to us and a trial that would give Clayton back his life. They were from India, as was a doctor that was following their son's situation. That being said, their doctor had discovered a seizure treatment utilizing ACTH (a steroid) that was not readily practiced within the United States (except with the condition of Infantile Spasms). High dosing of the steroid was administered, leveled off and then removed. This therapy showed promise in pediatric patients with intractable seizures, but it had its side effects, the most severe being loss of life due to adrenal hemorrhage. Tim and I didn't need to debate this option – we needed to try, for Clayton. We were thinking in the terms of "quality" rather than "quantity" of life by this point in Clayton's life and we needed to give him every chance of progress.

We knew Clayton's neurologist well, by this point, and she knew that we would not make any decision without thoroughly weighing the options. He was already inpatient, which was a prerequisite to start the therapy, so it was put in place. Were we nervous, that would be understatement. Though, we also knew that Clayton's life would not continue if the seizures were not controlled, and nothing would stop his seizures. Upon beginning the therapy, Clayton would have as many as 200 seizures a day. Obviously with that being said, we would try anything, and the therapy began. He was discharged from the hospital and we went home. At first, no evident signs of improvement were obvious. In fact, the only sign that he was on the therapy was that his entire body swelled. His little face was so swollen that it looked sore. Then, we began to see a change, so much so, that we started to videotape his progress. Seizures subsided and as they did, Clay became more coherent. He started to follow me with not only his eyes, as he was sitting in his wheelchair, but he would turn his head and body to see what I was doing. He started to play with his ball again and would even turn the pages of a book. One evening he was sitting on the couch (we had a recliner so that he could put his feet up) and he was studying my face as I was speaking to him. I put his hand to my mouth and slowly mouthed the word "mom." That is when our miracle occurred, Clayton spoke. He said, "Mom." I cried – tears of pure joy. I called my mother over, Tim was on a business trip and I wanted to make sure that I wasn't just sleep deprived when I heard him speak. I asked him to say it again and he did. When Tim arrived home, he couldn't believe the progress in the four days since he left. I didn't warn him, I wanted him to witness the miracle first hand, and I had Clayton speak. Tim was now the one in tears.

I wish I could say that Clayton's progress continued, but it didn't. Once the therapy was over, Clayton went back to countless seizures a day with no avail. He stopped speaking and eventually stopped playing. He still, though, retained the ability to give you a smile with a twinkle in his eyes that would melt your heart. Eventually, those moments became less frequent, but I always knew when Clayton was "there" by the look in his eyes.

I sat down one evening, exasperated, and knew that I had to do something. I was appalled that a condition such as Clay's was so misunderstood and lacked in resources. Epilepsy affected over 50 million individuals worldwide, at that time, and research and awareness were basically non-existent. I had an idea, which I flew with, and on my desktop computer I began a worldwide organization. Ashley helped me to select a name and "Clayton's Hope Organization" was formed. We had our first fundraiser that year, "Steps for Seizures," walk that she created for Epilepsy Research and Awareness. Ashley was able to present The Children's Hospital of Philadelphia's Epilepsy Program a check for $10,000 that year, to a room full of tear filled neurologists.

Our organization continued to grow and 2 years later my uncle introduced us to Road Scholar Transport. This wonderful company paints their trucks with the name and details of selected organizations. Through my uncle's tireless efforts, our truck was placed on the road in 2009, spreading Clayton's message across the United States. To date, our little organization has donated over $100,000 to Epilepsy Research and will continue to do so until a cure is found.

In March 2008, amidst the chaos of our life, we were blessed by two more miracles. Corrine and Gabriella entered our lives and completed our family. When they arrived home, not only did Ashley and Ashton hold their baby sisters, but we had Clayton hold them, as well. I picked up our newborns and placed them, one by one, on Clayton's lap. He wasn't able to hold them, so we positioned his arms around them and gave him the opportunity. They were born into a home of nurses, machines and a very sick brother – abnormal in anyone else's world, but everyday life in ours. They lived their young lives knowing that their brother was different, but to them, he was just their brother. Their world was very normal to them, as was Clayton.

Our world became more stable. Clayton attended a wonderful special needs school - we were blessed to have found such a group of caring teachers and enriching environment. He was loved, nurtured and never once treated as though he was "different" in any fashion. Although, he declined neurologically as time progressed, we still wanted him to have every opportunity to thrive. Even if he were alert for one moment in the day, we wanted that time to include all that a little boy should experience.

In addition to school, Clayton was also able to experience life through another blessing which arrived to our home. We received a phone call from the Make a Wish Foundation one afternoon informing us that Clayton had been chosen to receive a "wish". Anonymously, one of his nurses from his initial hospital stay wrote a letter and detailed his journey to the foundation. They gave us some options, one of which was Disney, but we wanted Clayton to fully enjoy his gift, and feared that he would end up staying in a hotel room. This was not a wish that Clayton, now, would enjoy. The hard part, was knowing what Clayton would want – without him being able to let us know. Tim and I, with the help of our family, sat down and tried to come up an idea which would give Clayton the greatest amount of joy – it came to us one evening. We made a video of Clayton the year before he got sick and gave it to each of the children, along with the grandparents – Ashton and Ashley loved this video of his brother so full of life. That was it, we were watching the video and realized that Clayton would be able to relive and, most of all, be a part of the world if he could see it better (our television was not exceedingly large). We made a phone call the next day and the foundation told us to pick out a large screen television, a stand to make it eye level for Clayton and surround sound so that he could experience the world. He did just that – the day that the television arrived we pushed his wheelchair in front of the screen and he watched in amazement. Clayton was now able to view the world, even though he was not able to physically journey to the places on the screen.

We learned how precious time is and the need for "family time". With the aid of our home nurses, we were able to allow our other children outings with both Tim and I – instead of one of us remaining at home. Clayton joined us, whenever his health allowed him to do so, but many times it was not possible. It was difficult not to take him, but as time went on and his condition declined, we had to give our other children the chance to have family memories. This process did not happen easily and I was riddled with guilt each time that we ventured out without Clayton in the beginning. Our family was not complete without him, but if I did not allow our other children to experience life, I knew I would look back at their childhoods with regret. I had to step back and realize that for some outings, Clayton was happier to home, and it eventually became less painful. Our children blossomed before our eyes, as we began to allow our lives to proceed. Ashley, who I always worried about the most, was thriving and living her life. She became a young woman who had maturity and self-confidence far beyond her years. Ashton grew into a young man who loved to play sports. He was extremely compassionate and affectionate towards everyone, especially his siblings. Corrine and Gabriella were amazing. They laughed and played and always included Clayton. Funny, they even blamed him for wrong doings that he couldn't possibly have performed – but, in their eyes he could do anything that they were capable of doing.

I went back to work part - time for the company which we utilized for Clayton's nursing/medical equipment. I was able to utilize my experiences to help others by transitioning home medically fragile children from the hospital. My mother stayed home and aided us, once again, by watching our children 3 days a week while I worked. Ashley went off to college and followed her dream of art. Tim continued in a position which he loved. Ashton, Corrine and Gabriella were busy in school and sports. Our lives became "normal" and were no longer "out of bubble" – we were living and enjoying every minute.

In April 2012, though, our dreams of a happy ending came to an end. Clay became sick again. He was admitted to the hospital three times within a two month period and was inpatient for all of 2 weeks. The seizures would not stop this time and the virus, which began our journey, seemed to have returned. On one of the trips back to the hospital, Clayton almost didn't make it. Upon arriving at the hospital, the medical team had to call a "code blue" and whisk him into the resuscitation room. I watched in horror as they worked on him. Clayton, though, surprised everyone and stabilized. He spent 2 weeks in the hospital on that occasion. Though, 3 days after being discharged, we had to call 911. He was transported back to the hospital. Looking back, that last trip probably was foreshadowing. The EMT's called for a police escort, which had never transpired previously, and all lanes were cleared into Philadelphia for Clayton. This time would be different – they could not make him well. He had declined steadily during those 3 months. Many of the same events transpired, but in the end, Clayton told us in his own way that he was tired and couldn't fight any longer. We no longer were fighting for Clayton, we were doing so for ourselves; therefore, we did the last thing that we could for our son. We let go of our reigns and put it in Clayton and God's hands.

We brought him home from the hospital, read him stories, played his favorite music and welcomed friends and family who wished to visit him. We had the opportunity to tell him everything that was in our hearts and the difference that he made in our lives. Ashley, Ashton, Corrine and Gabriella were able to say goodbye. When it was time for Clay to leave to us - Tim and I told him to go to the beach; to walk in the sand, to meet up with his family and friends who went to heaven before him; to not be scared. I told him that he could let go of my hand and not look back. I told him to not stay and linger after he passed, to go into a wonderful place and that we will be together again. I know in my heart for this to be the case. On August 4, 2012, Clayton passed away peaceful in my arms.

Clayton made more of a difference in his lifetime, than most adults will in their entire lives – we told him this the night that he became an angel. He brought out the best in people and allowed us to help others in our situation. He continues to help us make a difference each day. It was never as evident as the day of his funeral. During the procession, led by Road Scholar's Clayton's Hope 18 wheel truck, people stopped and watched. Individuals held signs along the road, they waved from their cars and his school set up a celebration (Tim had the wonderful idea of stopping at the school to allow the staff/children to say goodbye). The school made signs, had music playing, wore bright colors and the students even signed the truck. They celebrated Clay that day and his life that he shared with so many. Though he was never able to speak after the illness, he spoke volumes and spread his message to the world.

I hold dear our memories over the eight years of his illness, because we were blessed to have those years with Clay. Were they easy? Not in the slightest bit. It was a journey that was physically, emotionally and mentally devastating. We watched, we learned, we sometimes listened and very often cried. The stress brought out both the best and worst of my personality and I am externally grateful for my husband, our children, my parents, our family, friends, nurses, the hospital personnel and our community - for the love and support that I was given.

Our children are continuing their lives, as they should. I see Clay in each of them and I know that they each contain parts of his personality within their souls. I believe that they will each be more compassionate with those less fortunate and have a greater empathy for those in need. The scars have begun to heal and somehow they seem well adjusted. They will, of course, ask about Clay very often. Each of them has their own way of missing him and we let them. We include Clay in all that we do because he will always be a member of our family. We gave each of our children a present from Clay, the morning that they awoke to find him gone. Tim and I let them know that Clay became an angel, but he wanted to leave something he treasured, with each of them, so that they could hold it whenever they needed him. To this day, they do. I don't make them talk, I just try and listen and be as strong as I am able at the moment. I cannot take credit for their unbelievable adjustment; it was achieved due to many individuals.

I am given signs regularly that he approves and is whole again. I know in my heart that he is doing all of the things that his body would not allow him to do any longer on Earth. I am privileged to be his voice through our charity, my occupation, the State of New Jersey Epilepsy Task Force (which I am honored to serve) and those who will read this book. Mostly, I am humbled and honored to be blessed to parent five wonderful children. When asked how many children I have, my response will forever be the same, "five" - one is just eternally 14.